ALL-IN-ONE OVEN MEALS

ALL-IN-ONE

RUTH BEAN

OVEN MEALS

Publishers • Bramhall House • New York

This edition is published by Bramhall House, a division of Clarkson N. Potter, Inc. by arrangement with the original publishers M. Barrows, Inc.

(A)

Manufactured in the United States of America
by H. Wolff, New York

With real affection
to "Ruthie" Kamper
my devoted assistant on television. Without
her unfailing interest, help, and prodding,
this book might never have been written.

Contents

Foreword

ALL-IN-ONE OVEN MEALS has been written with today's busy woman in mind. You will find in these pages simple, moderately-priced, delicious meals . . . recipes which have been carefully tested and written so the newest cook, as well as the expert, can serve meals of which she can be proud.

The art of oven and broiler cookery has been much overlooked. The woman who has discovered this art will tell you it keeps her kitchen cool and uncluttered and leaves her free to be the charming wife, mother and hostess. The business girl will find this method of cooking truly magical.

A proper oven meal consists of foods that can be cooked in the oven at the same time and temperature. When the oven is to be used for one dish, it makes for a greater economy of time, effort and money to place in it as many other dishes as possible. Oven-cooked meals demand little attention, and so give the women of today many more leisure hours.

Certain cakes and pastries cannot be oven-cooked together with other foods. Added moisture in the oven is unsuitable for delicate cakes and crisp pastries, but moist cakes—spice, applesauce, gingerbread—and puddings may be baked along with other foods. Crisp breads like cornsticks are taboo.

However, there are hundreds of foods which are adaptable to this type of cookery. Many of your own favorite recipes may be substituted for those I have given, but I do respectfully request that you first try these recipes exactly as given, and use the correct-size pans, before you branch out on your own.

Special Note: All recipes containing baking powder are based on the double-action type. If cream-of-tartar baking powder is used, please increase the amounts given by one-third. This is of particular importance in cold-oven-start meals, or where foods are prepared in advance and refrigerated for later cooking.

Part I of this book is devoted to dishes to be placed in a preheated oven. Foods may be prepared in advance and refrigerated until cooking time. Do not hesitate to move glass baking dishes from the refrigerator into a hot oven. The temperature difference between refrigerator and room is rarely more than 40 degrees, but there may be 400 degrees difference between room and oven temperature. The additional 40 degrees will not matter.

In planning an oven meal it is always wise to place the pans to be used in the oven to make sure they will fit without touching each other or the sides of the oven. If pans touch anything, burning may result. The pan sizes given fit an average-size oven.

Part II will take you into the field of cold oven-start meals. This method is particularly satisfactory with clock-controlled ovens. The foods may all be prepared in advance, refrigerated until well chilled, then placed in a cold oven. If the oven is insulated, foods will not spoil even on the hottest day. After all, if 400 degrees of heat cannot get out into the room, surely 90 degrees room heat cannot get into the insulated oven. All cold-start meals can be placed in a preheated oven if desired. Reduce baking time indicated by 15 minutes when oven is preheated.

Part III is concerned with broiler meals, the quickest of all to prepare. They are usually also slightly more expensive, as only tender cuts of meat may be used. The meals in this book have been planned with your budget in mind.

The index lists menus that require 30 minutes or less cooking, those that take 60 minutes or less, and those requiring more than 60 minutes oven time.

Just a word to the wise. If you do not like to scrub your oven, always make sure that roasts are in a pan small enough so the fat will not dry out and fry, causing it to spatter. Meat should never be more than two inches from sides of pan. If an oven becomes greasy or spill-overs do occur, clean at once. If foods burn on, simply raise the oven temperature to 550 degrees until they char and can be easily removed.

It is my sincere hope that these meals will give you many pleasant hours around your table and more time for your hobbies.

Ramsey   *Ruth Bean*
New Jersey
August, 1952

I

INTO A HOT OVEN

Menu 1. Avocado and Creamed Crab for Four

(40-MINUTE OVEN TIME)

AVOCADO AND CREAMED CRAB

CELERY   RADISHES   SLICED TOMATOES

APPLE MUFFINS AND BUTTER

COTTAGE PUDDING WITH ORANGE SAUCE   TEA

Avocado and Creamed Crab

2 avocados
2 tablespoons lemon juice
3 tablespoons butter
3 tablespoons flour
¼ teaspoon dry mustard
¼ teaspoon onion juice

¼ teaspoon salt
⅛ teaspoon pepper
1 cup milk
1 cup crab meat
2 hard-cooked eggs, chopped

Cut avocados in half; do not peel. Remove stones and brush cut surface with lemon juice. Melt butter; stir in flour and seasonings until smooth. Add milk slowly, stirring constantly until mixture thickens. Stir in crab meat and chopped egg. Pack creamed mixture into avocado halves.

CRUMBS

½ cup soft bread crumbs
¼ cup grated cheese

3 tablespoons melted butter

Combine all ingredients and blend well. Spread over creamed crab in avocados. Place stuffed avocado halves in baking pan. Pour warm water around avocados to a 1-inch depth.

Apple Muffins

2 cups all-purpose flour
¾ teaspoon salt
4 teaspoons baking powder
¼ cup sugar
¾ teaspoon cinnamon
¼ teaspoon nutmeg

1 egg, beaten
1 cup milk
⅓ cup melted shortening
¾ cup chopped apples, pared
    and cored

Sift together flour, salt, baking powder, sugar, cinnamon and nutmeg. Combine beaten egg, milk and melted shortening; pour over dry ingredients and stir until they are just moistened. Stir in chopped apples. Grease muffin pans and fill ⅔ full with batter.

Cottage Pudding

1½ cups cake flour
¼ teaspoon salt
2 teaspoons baking powder
⅔ cup sugar

1 egg, beaten
½ cup milk
½ teaspoon vanilla
⅓ cup melted shortening

Sift together flour, salt, baking powder and sugar. Combine beaten egg, milk and vanilla. Blend together sifted ingredients and egg mixture; add melted shortening and beat well. Pour batter into greased 8-inch-square baking pan.

ORANGE SAUCE

½ cup sugar
1½ tablespoons cornstarch
⅛ teaspoon salt

1 cup orange juice
2 tablespoons butter

Combine sugar, cornstarch and salt; stir in orange juice. Cook, while stirring, over medium heat until clear and thickened; stir in butter. Serve hot over the baked cottage pudding.

Baking Directions

Preheat oven to moderate 350° F. Place avocados on lower shelf. Place muffins and cottage pudding on shelf above. Bake 40 minutes.

Menu 2. Crab-Cheese Casserole
for Four
(90-MINUTE OVEN TIME)

CRAB-CHEESE CASSEROLE

BUTTERED LIMA BEANS

TOSSED VEGETABLE SALAD

COCONUT PUDDING   HARD SAUCE   COFFEE

Crab-Cheese Casserole

6 slices white bread with crusts   2¼ cups milk
2 tablespoons butter   ½ teaspoon salt
1 can crab meat   ⅛ teaspoon pepper
1½ cups grated Cheddar cheese   ¼ teaspoon prepared mustard
3 eggs   ¼ cup sherry wine

Butter bread and cut each slice into 4 long strips. Alternate layers
of bread, crab and cheese in greased 2-quart casserole. Beat eggs;
add milk, salt, pepper, mustard and sherry. Blend. Pour over
crab mixture. Place casserole in pan of water and bake.

Buttered Lima Beans

1 package frozen Lima beans   ⅛ teaspoon pepper
½ cup water   2 tablespoons butter
¼ teaspoon salt

Place all ingredients in saucepan; cover tightly.

Coconut Pudding

¼ cup butter   30 large graham crackers
⅓ cup sugar   ¼ teaspoon salt
1 egg, separated   1¼ teaspoons baking powder
¾ cup shredded coconut   1¼ cups milk
1 teaspoon vanilla

Cream butter and sugar; add egg yolk and beat until fluffy. Stir in coconut and vanilla. Crush graham crackers very fine and add salt and baking powder. Add alternately with milk to creamed mixture. Fold in beaten egg white. Pour into greased loaf pan. Serve with hard sauce.

HARD SAUCE

⅓ cup butter
1 cup confectioners sugar

1 teaspoon vanilla
⅛ teaspoon nutmeg

Cream butter; add sugar slowly, creaming thoroughly. Add vanilla and nutmeg and blend. Chill 30 minutes or longer before serving.

Baking Directions

Preheat oven to moderate 325° F. Place crab meat on lower shelf. At the end of 30 minutes baking, place Lima beans on shelf with crab meat; on shelf directly above place coconut pudding. Bake 1 hour longer. Total oven time 90 minutes.

Delicious Extra: Tossed Vegetable Salad

1½ cups torn, not cut, salad
  greens
3 tablespoons salad oil
6 radishes, sliced thin
1 small onion, sliced thin
2 tomatoes, coarsely diced
½ cup cold cooked vegetables
1 egg
¼ teaspoon dry mustard

¼ teaspoon salt
½ teaspoon sugar
⅛ teaspoon pepper
¼ teaspoon paprika
1 tablespoon vinegar
1 slice white bread
1 clove garlic, peeled and cut in
  half

Pour salad oil over greens and add vegetables. Toss gently until all are coated with oil. Add raw egg and blend. Combine the mustard, salt, sugar, pepper, paprika and vinegar, and pour over salad mixture. Rub bread with garlic and cut in very small pieces; add to salad and toss well, being careful not to bruise greens. Chill before serving.

Menu 3. Speedy Crab Dinner for Four
(25-MINUTE OVEN TIME)

MOCK CLAM SHELLS WITH CRAB

ANCHOVY-STUFFED CELERY   PEAS IN CREAM

CORN BREAD   BUTTER

BRANDIED WATERMELON   TEA

Mock Clam Shells with Crab

3 cups fine cracker crumbs   ¼ cup butter, melted

Blend cracker crumbs and butter. Divide into 8 mounds on greased cooky sheet. Shape into clam shells. Fill with crab meat mixture and bake.

CRAB MEAT FILLING

¼ cup butter	2 tablespoons chopped chives
¼ cup flour	1¼ cups milk
¼ teaspoon salt	1 egg yolk
⅛ teaspoon pepper	2 cups flaked crab meat
⅛ teaspoon dry mustard	⅓ cup grated Cheddar cheese

Melt butter; add flour, salt, pepper, mustard and chives. Stir until smooth; add milk slowly and cook until smooth and thickened. Add beaten egg yolk and crab meat. Pack into mock shells. Top with grated cheese and bake.

Peas in Cream

2 tablespoons butter	1 package frozen peas
2 tablespoons water	2 tablespoons cream
¼ teaspoon sugar	⅛ teaspoon salt

Place butter, water and sugar in saucepan; add peas and cover tightly. Before serving, add cream and salt, and toss lightly to season.

Corn Bread

¾ cup corn-meal muffin mix   1 egg
¾ cup biscuit mix   1¼ cups milk
2 tablespoons sugar

Blend muffin mix and biscuit mix; add sugar. Beat egg and add milk. Add milk and egg to flour mixture. Stir until smooth. Pour into greased 9-inch-square pan and bake.

Baking Directions

Preheat oven to hot, 425° F. Place filled shells on lower shelf; on shelf directly above, place corn bread and peas. Bake everything 25 minutes.

Crispy Addition: Anchovy-Stuffed Celery

3-ounce package cream cheese   ¼ teaspoon Worcestershire
1 tablespoon anchovy paste   sauce
                                 8 stalks celery

Blend softened cheese, anchovy paste and Worcestershire sauce; pack into celery stalks and chill.

Tasty Dessert: Brandied Watermelon

1 small watermelon   ¼ cup brandy

Cut triangular one-inch plug from melon. Pour in brandy. Replace plug. Roll melon around. Chill, cut and serve.

Menu 4. Lobster Bridge Supper for Eight
(30-MINUTE OVEN TIME)

Lobster with Cheese Swirls

⅓ cup chopped onion
½ cup chopped green pepper
½ cup butter
1 teaspoon salt
¾ cup flour
4 egg yolks, beaten

1 can condensed mushroom
  soup
3 cups milk
3 cans (8-ounce) lobster meat
½ cup sherry wine

Slowly cook onion and green pepper in butter until soft. Do not brown. Add salt and flour, and blend. Mix egg yolks, soup and milk, and slowly add to flour mixture, stirring until sauce thickens. Pick over lobster meat; remove any shell. Add with sherry to cream sauce. Pour into greased 9- by 15-inch baking pan.

CHEESE SWIRLS

3 cups sifted all-purpose flour
2 teaspoons baking powder
¾ teaspoon salt
1 tablespoon sugar
6 tablespoons shortening

1 cup milk
1 cup grated Cheddar cheese
½ cup chopped stuffed olives
⅛ teaspoon cayenne pepper

Sift together flour, baking powder, salt and sugar. Cut in shortening, add milk and mix. Roll on floured cloth into large rectangle ¼ inch thick. Sprinkle with cheese, olives and cayenne. Roll lengthwise. Slice ¾ inch thick and place slices, cut side up, over lobster.

Tart Shells

2⅔ cups all-purpose flour
½ teaspoon salt

1 cup shortening
½ cup cold water

Blend flour and salt. Cut in shortening; add water. Blend with a fork. Roll pastry; cut 8 six-inch rounds. Fit over large inverted muffin pans. Pinch into shape. Prick well with fork.

Meringues

4 egg whites
¼ cup cold water

½ cup sugar
1 tablespoon lemon juice

Beat egg whites and water together until stiff. Slowly beat in sugar and lemon juice. Beat until very stiff. Pour ½ inch of hot water into each of 8 greased muffin cups. Place some meringue mixture on top of water in each pan. Bake in oven for 20 minutes on heat left after removing dinner.

STRAWBERRY FILLING

1½ quarts strawberries

1 cup confectioners sugar

Wash, hull and slice berries. Toss with sugar and pile into cooled tart shells. Top with meringues lifted carefully from water. Serve at once.

Baking Directions

Preheat oven to very hot, 475° F. Place lobster covered with cheese swirls on lower shelf. On shelf directly above, place tart shells. After 15 minutes baking time, remove tart shells and bake lobster 15 minutes longer. Total oven time 30 minutes.

Menu 5. Lobster Tails for Four
(30-MINUTE OVEN TIME)

BAKED LOBSTER TAILS

FRENCH FRIED POTATOES

FRESH ASPARAGUS   LEMON BUTTER SAUCE

FRESH STRAWBERRY COFFEECAKE   COFFEE

Baked Lobster Tails

2 lobster tails, about 1¼ pounds each
¼ cup butter, melted
1 tablespoon lemon juice
¼ teaspoon salt
⅛ teaspoon pepper
⅛ teaspoon orégano
½ cup grated Cheddar cheese

Wash lobster tails. Split in half lengthwise and place in greased baking pan. Melt butter and add lemon juice, salt, pepper and orégano. Pour over lobster tails. Top each with grated cheese.

French Fried Potatoes

1 package frozen French fried potatoes
¼ teaspoon salt

Spread out potatoes in baking pan so they do not overlap. Sprinkle with salt before serving.

Fresh Asparagus

1 bunch fresh asparagus
1 cup water
¼ teaspoon salt

Cut off tough part of stalks. Wash thoroughly to remove sand. Place in loaf pan. Add water and salt. Cover pan tightly with aluminum foil.

LEMON BUTTER SAUCE

⅓ cup butter   1 tablespoon lemon juice
2 tablespoons hot water   ⅛ teaspoon pepper

Melt butter; add hot water, lemon juice and pepper. Serve over asparagus.

Fresh Strawberry Coffeecake

2 cups sifted all-purpose flour   1 egg, beaten
2 teaspoons baking powder   1½ cups fresh strawberries
⅓ cup sugar   ¼ cup sugar
½ teaspoon salt   3 tablespoons flour
⅓ cup shortening   ½ teaspoon nutmeg
⅓ cup milk   3 tablespoons soft butter

Sift together the flour, baking powder, sugar and salt. Cut in shortening. Combine milk and beaten egg and add to flour mixture. Blend with fork. Pat to cover 10- x 6-inch greased pan. Arrange fresh strawberries over dough. Blend together ¼ cup sugar, 3 tablespoons flour, nutmeg and soft butter to form crumbs. Sprinkle crumbs over strawberries.

Baking Directions

Preheat oven to hot, 400° F. Place lobster and asparagus on lower shelf. On shelf directly above, place strawberry cake and potatoes. Bake 30 minutes.

Menu 6. Fresh Lobster for the Gang
(20-MINUTE OVEN TIME)

LOBSTER WITH SHERRY CRUMBS

CELERY, OLIVES AND PICKLES

POTATO CHIPS   HOT GARLIC BREAD

BAKED TOMATOES

BANANA-RASPBERRY BAVARIAN CREAM   COFFEE

Lobster with Sherry Crumbs for Twelve

12 two-pound boiled lobsters	¼ teaspoon pepper
½ pound butter, melted	3 tablespoons melted butter
⅓ cup lemon juice	¼ cup sherry wine
½ teaspoon salt	1½ cups soft bread crumbs

Open lobsters over sink to get rid of liquid. Grease a 3-quart casserole. Remove lobster meat from body, claws and legs. Cut larger pieces of meat to serving size. Work over casserole to catch all the green lobster fat and the coral or roe. Melt ½ pound butter; add lemon juice, salt and pepper. Pour over lobster. Combine 3 tablespoons melted butter and sherry wine. Pour slowly over bread crumbs. Toss until all are moistened. Sprinkle over lobster; cover tightly.

Hot Garlic Bread

1 large loaf French bread	⅓ cup butter
1 clove garlic	

Slice French bread almost through to lower crust. Cut garlic clove and rub over surface of small mixing bowl. Cream butter in garlic-rubbed bowl. Spread slices of bread generously. Spread remaining butter over top of loaf. Place in baking pan.

Baked Tomatoes

12 large tomatoes
1 teaspoon salt
¼ teaspoon pepper
1¾ cups dry bread crumbs

1 tablespoon onion juice
¼ cup grated Parmesan cheese
¼ cup melted butter

Wash tomatoes. Cut in half. Salt and pepper each half. Mix together crumbs, onion juice, cheese and butter. Pack on tomato halves. Place on cooky sheet.

Baking Directions

Preheat oven to 400° F. Place lobster and garlic bread on lower shelf. On shelf directly above, place tomatoes. Bake 20 minutes.

Banana-Raspberry Bavarian Cream

1 package raspberry gelatine
1 cup hot water
1 package frozen raspberries
1 cup drained raspberry juice
    and water

2 bananas, diced
½ cup heavy cream, whipped
24 ladyfingers

Dissolve gelatine in hot water. Thaw raspberries and drain off juice. Measure juice and add water to make 1 cup. Stir into dissolved gelatine. Chill until slightly thickened. Beat with egg beater until fluffy. Fold in berries, bananas and whipped cream. Line 1½-quart casserole with ladyfingers. Pour over Bavarian cream. Chill until firm. Serve in pie-shaped wedges.

Menu 7. Scallops and Mushrooms for Four
(35-MINUTE OVEN TIME)

BAKED SCALLOPS AND MUSHROOMS

SCALLIONS AND RADISHES

POTATO PUFFS

GREEN BEANS IN ONION BUTTER

MOCHA BROWNIES   STRAWBERRY ICE CREAM   COFFEE

Baked Scallops and Mushrooms

1 pint bay scallops	½ teaspoon salt
2 cups boiling water	⅛ teaspoon pepper
1 pound fresh mushrooms	1 cup milk
½ cup butter	⅓ cup bread crumbs
3 tablespoons flour	

Wash scallops to remove sand. Cut across the grain in thin slices. Drop into boiling water and simmer 10 minutes. Drain, wash and slice mushrooms. Melt butter. Brown mushrooms lightly for 5 minutes, and carefully remove from pan. To the butter in the frying pan add flour, salt and pepper. Stir until smooth. Slowly add milk and cook, stirring constantly, until thickened. Combine drained scallops, mushrooms and sauce. Pour into greased 1½-quart casserole and top with crumbs.

Potato Puffs

2 packages frozen potato puffs   ¼ teaspoon salt

Place potato puffs in shallow baking pan. Before serving, season with salt.

Green Beans in Onion Butter

2½ cups (No. 2 can) green beans
3 tablespoons melted butter

1 teaspoon onion juice
⅛ teaspoon pepper

Drain beans. Place in 1-quart casserole. Blend butter, onion juice and pepper. Pour over beans. Cover tightly.

Mocha Brownies

½ cup butter
1 cup sugar
1 teaspoon instant coffee
2 eggs
2 one-ounce squares bitter chocolate, melted

⅔ cup all-purpose flour
½ teaspoon salt
1 teaspoon vanilla
⅔ cup chopped walnuts

Cream butter, sugar and coffee. Add eggs, one at a time, beating thoroughly. Add cooled melted chocolate. Add flour and salt. Blend until smooth. Stir in vanilla and nuts. Pack into 11- by 7-inch greased pan.

Baking Directions

Preheat oven to moderate, 350° F. Place potatoes and beans on lower shelf. On shelf directly above, place brownies and scallops. Bake everything 35 minutes.

Sweet Finish: Strawberry Ice Cream

1 pint strawberries
⅔ cup sugar
1 egg

⅓ cup sugar
1 pint heavy cream

Wash, drain and stem strawberries. Mash and add ⅔ cup sugar. Beat egg until lemon colored. Add ⅓ cup sugar and 1 cup cream. Combine berries and egg mixture. Pour into freezer tray and freeze firm. Whip remaining 1 cup cream. Remove frozen berry mixture and spoon into chilled bowl. Beat until smooth. Fold in whipped cream and return to freezer. Freeze firm, about 2 hours.

Menu 8. Striped Bass Dinner for Six
(50-MINUTE OVEN TIME)

BAKED STUFFED STRIPED BASS

TOMATO CASSEROLE   COLESLAW WITH SOUR CREAM

RYE BREAD AND BUTTER

PEACH PANDOWDY   COFFEE

Baked Striped Bass

1 three-pound striped bass, split   4 tablespoons melted butter
  and cleaned   Salt and pepper

Wipe fish with damp cloth and place, skin side down, on greased baking dish. Brush well with melted butter and sprinkle with salt and pepper.

STUFFING

¼ cup chopped celery   1 to 1½ cups cooked rice
¼ cup chopped onion   2 tablespoons chopped parsley
2 tablespoons butter

Brown celery and onion lightly in butter; combine with rice and parsley. Blend well and spread over fish. Top with these in this order:

1 can condensed mushroom   1 medium-sized onion, sliced
  soup, diluted with   2 tablespoons grated cheese
½ can water

Tomato Casserole

½ cup bread crumbs   ¼ cup chopped green pepper
2½ cups (No. 2 can) tomatoes   1 small onion, chopped
2 tablespoons sugar   1 tablespoon butter
Salt and pepper

Sprinkle half the bread crumbs over bottom of greased 1-quart casserole. Combine tomatoes, sugar, seasonings, green pepper and onion, and turn into casserole. Top with remaining bread crumbs. Dot with butter.

Peach Pandowdy

2 cups canned sliced peaches	2 tablespoons butter
½ cup sugar	1 cup heavy cream, whipped
¼ teaspoon cinnamon	

Line bottom of greased 9-inch-square cake pan with sliced peaches. Sprinkle with sugar and cinnamon, and dot with butter. Cover with batter mixture. Bake and serve warm with whipped cream.

BATTER

¼ cup shortening	1½ teaspoons baking powder
⅔ cup sugar	1½ cups all-purpose flour
1 egg, separated	¼ teaspoon salt
½ teaspoon vanilla	½ cup milk

Cream shortening and sugar; add egg yolk and vanilla, and blend well. Sift baking powder, flour and salt together and add alternately with milk to creamed mixture. Beat egg white until stiff but not dry; fold carefully into first mixture. Pour batter over peaches.

Baking Directions

Preheat oven to moderate, 350° F. Place bass and tomatoes on lower shelf. Place pandowdy in center of shelf directly above. At the end of 40 minutes, remove bass and tomatoes. Bake pandowdy 10 minutes longer. Total oven time 50 minutes.

Good Accompaniment: Coleslaw with Sour Cream

1 small head cabbage, shredded	1 pimento, chopped
¼ cup chopped green pepper	1 carrot, finely grated
2 tablespoons finely chopped onion	

Soak shredded cabbage in ice water for 15 minutes. Drain and combine with remaining chilled ingredients.

DRESSING

3 tablespoons lemon juice	¼ teaspoon salt
¾ cup sour cream	1 teaspoon prepared mustard
2 tablespoons sugar	

Thoroughly blend all ingredients and chill. When ready to serve, fold carefully into shredded cabbage mixture.

Menu 9. Bluefish Dinner for Six
(45-MINUTE OVEN TIME)

TUNA COCKTAIL   CELERY
BAKED BLUEFISH WITH MUSHROOM SAUCE
VEGETABLE RING   FRENCH FRIED POTATOES
ALMOND-PECAN CAKE   PEACH ICE CREAM   COFFEE

Baked Bluefish with Mushroom Sauce

1 three-pound bluefish, cleaned
   and boned
¼ pound mushrooms, sliced
1 small onion, chopped
⅓ cup boiling water
3 tablespoons butter

3 tablespoons flour
½ teaspoon salt
¼ teaspoon pepper
2 cups milk
½ teaspoon paprika

Place bluefish in large, greased baking pan. Cook sliced mushrooms and chopped onion in boiling water for 3 minutes; add butter, flour, salt, pepper and milk, and bring to a boil, stirring constantly. Pour sauce over fish in baking pan and sprinkle with paprika.

Vegetable Ring

3 eggs, well beaten
1 cup milk
3 cups mixed cooked vegetables
1 tablespoon finely-chopped
   onion

1 tablespoon chopped parsley
1 teaspoon salt
¼ teaspoon pepper

Combine ingredients in order given. Pour into greased 1-quart ring mold.

French Fried Potatoes

2 packages frozen French fried
   potatoes

1 teaspoon salt

Place frozen potatoes in large greased baking pan so that they do not overlap. Sprinkle with salt.

Almond-Pecan Cake

¾ cup shortening
2 cups sugar
3 eggs
3 cups sifted all-purpose flour
1½ teaspoons baking soda
1 teaspoon salt

1½ cups buttermilk
½ teaspoon almond flavoring
1½ teaspoons lemon juice
3 ounces unsweetened chocolate, melted
⅓ cup chopped pecans

Cream shortening and sugar thoroughly; add unbeaten eggs, one at a time, beating well after each addition. Sift together flour, baking soda and salt, and add alternately with buttermilk. Stir in almond flavoring, lemon juice and melted chocolate cooled; fold in chopped pecans. Pour batter into greased oblong baking pan, about 9 by 12 inches.

Baking Directions

Preheat oven to moderate, 350° F. Place bluefish on lower shelf; place vegetable ring and almond-pecan cake on shelf directly above. At the end of 15 minutes baking time, place potatoes on shelf with bluefish and continue baking 30 minutes longer. Total baking time 45 minutes.

Good Beginning: Tuna Cocktail

6 crisp lettuce leaves
1 seven-ounce can tuna, chunk-style
⅓ head lettuce, cut in small chunks
¼ cup diced celery

3 tablespoons Worcestershire sauce
⅛ teaspoon Tabasco sauce
1 tablespoon horse-radish sauce
⅔ cup tomato catsup
¼ cup lemon juice
6 parsley springs

Place a lettuce leaf in each of six cocktail glasses. Combine tuna chunks, lettuce and celery, and place in glasses. Blend Worcestershire, Tabasco, horse-radish, catsup, lemon juice; pour over tuna mixture and top each serving with sprig of parsley. Chill and serve.

Menu 10. Haddock Fillets for Six
(25-MINUTE OVEN TIME)

ROLLED HADDOCK FILLETS WITH EGG SAUCE
GLAZED CARROTS   BUTTERED SUCCOTASH
GRAHAM MUFFINS   BUTTER   ORANGE MARMALADE
LEMON SHERBET   VANILLA WAFERS *   COFFEE

* (Buy these.)

Rolled Haddock Fillets

6 haddock fillets
1 teaspoon salt
1½ cups soft bread crumbs
1 tablespoon grated onion
2 tablespoons chopped parsley

¼ teaspoon salt
⅛ teaspoon pepper
¼ cup milk
2 tablespoons butter

Wipe haddock and rub with salt. Make a dressing by mixing bread crumbs, onion, parsley, salt, pepper and milk. Spread on fish. Roll stuffed fillets. Fasten with toothpicks. Place in greased baking pan. Spread with butter.

EGG SAUCE

4 tablespoons butter
4 tablespoons flour
Dash of pepper

1 teaspoon salt
2 cups milk
3 hard-cooked eggs, chopped

Make a medium white sauce with the first five ingredients and stir in hard-cooked eggs.

Glazed Carrots

12 small cooked carrots
¼ cup sugar
¼ cup butter, melted

¼ cup hot water
¼ teaspoon salt

Place carrots in saucepan. Combine sugar, butter, water and salt; pour over carrots. Cover tightly.

Buttered Succotash

1 package frozen succotash
½ cup water
¼ teaspoon salt

⅛ teaspoon pepper
2 tablespoons butter

Place succotash and water in saucepan. Cover tightly. Before serving, drain and season with salt, pepper and butter.

Graham Muffins

1½ cups graham flour
3 tablespoons sugar
1 teaspoon salt
1 teaspoon baking soda

1 tablespoon molasses
1 cup buttermilk
¼ cup melted butter

Mix (do not sift) flour, sugar, salt and soda together. Add molasses, buttermilk and butter. Stir to moisten. Do not beat smooth. Grease 12 muffin cups; fill ⅔ full.

Baking Directions

Preheat oven to hot, 425° F. Place carrots and succotash on lower shelf. On shelf directly above, place fish and muffins. Bake everything 25 minutes.

Refreshing Ending: Lemon Sherbet

¼ cup lemon juice
1 teaspoon grated lemon rind
2 cups sugar

2 cups milk
1 pint heavy cream

Heat lemon juice. Add rind and sugar, and stir until sugar is dissolved. Add milk and pour into freezer tray. Freeze. Whip cream. Mash and whip lemon base. Fold into whipped cream and return to refrigerator and freeze. Makes 2 quarts.

Menu 11. Halibut Soufflé for Eight
(90-MINUTE OVEN TIME)

HALIBUT SOUFFLÉ WITH LOBSTER SAUCE
CELERY, OLIVES AND PICKLES
WHIPPED POTATOES   ASPARAGUS WITH BUTTER
ORANGE BREAD PUDDING   COFFEE

Halibut Soufflé

2 cups cream
2½ cups soft bread crumbs
1 tablespoon butter
½ teaspoon salt
⅛ teaspoon pepper
¼ teaspoon celery salt
1½ pounds chopped raw
   halibut
4 egg whites

Scald cream. *Do not boil.* Add bread crumbs, butter, salt, pepper and celery salt. Add chopped halibut and cook slowly until thoroughly heated. *Do not boil.* Fold in stiffly beaten egg whites. Pour in greased 2½-quart casserole. Set in pan of hot water.

LOBSTER SAUCE

3 tablespoons butter
3 tablespoons flour
1 teaspoon salt
⅛ teaspoon pepper
1 cup milk
½ cup heavy cream
1½ cups fresh lobster
½ cup crushed cheese crackers

Melt butter; add flour, salt and pepper. Add milk and cook until smooth and thickened, stirring constantly. Add cream and lobster and heat *Do not boil.* Serve over halibut. Sprinkle with crushed cheese crackers.

Whipped Potatoes

8 large potatoes
1 cup water
½ teaspoon salt

¼ cup butter
¼ cup hot milk
¼ teaspoon pepper

Pare and slice potatoes. Place in saucepan with water and salt. Cover tightly. Before serving mash and season with butter, milk and pepper. Whip until fluffy.

Asparagus

2 packages frozen asparagus
¾ cup water
¼ teaspoon salt

⅛ teaspoon pepper
¼ cup melted butter

Place frozen asparagus and water in saucepan. Cover tightly. Before serving season with salt, pepper and melted butter.

Orange Bread Pudding

4 egg yolks
¼ cup sugar
¼ teaspoon salt
1 tablespoon butter, melted
2 teaspoons grated orange rind

1 teaspoon grated lemon rind
¾ cup orange juice
1 cup evaporated milk
2 cups day-old bread cubes
½ cup raisins

Beat egg yolks; add sugar, salt, melted butter, orange rind, lemon rind, orange juice and milk. Pour over bread. Add raisins and mix well. Pour into greased loaf pan and set in pan of warm water. When serving garnish, if desired, with fresh orange segments and currant jelly.

Baking Directions

Preheat oven to moderate, 350° F. Place halibut and potatoes on lower shelf. On shelf directly above, place pudding and asparagus. Bake everything 90 minutes.

Menu 12. Friday Salmon Special for Four

(35-MINUTE OVEN TIME)

SALMON CASSEROLE

OVEN-CREAMED POTATOES   BROCCOLI

CRISP SALAD GREENS WITH CUCUMBER SOUR-CREAM DRESSING (MENU 61)

APRICOT COBBLER   COFFEE

Salmon Casserole

¼ cup butter
2 teaspoons onion, finely chopped
1½ cups fine soft bread crumbs
½ teaspoon salt
⅛ teaspoon pepper

1-pound can red salmon
1 cup salmon liquor plus milk
1 teaspoon lemon juice
¼ teaspoon grated lemon rind
1 tablespoon chopped parsley
1 egg, beaten

Melt butter, add onion and cook until lightly browned. Add bread crumbs and toss until all of the butter is absorbed. Add salt and pepper and brown crumbs slightly. Drain salmon liquor into cup and add milk to make 1 cup. Skin, bone and flake salmon. Combine all ingredients and pour into greased 1½-quart casserole.

Oven-Creamed Potatoes

¼ cup butter
¼ cup flour
½ teaspoon salt
¼ teaspoon dry mustard
⅛ teaspoon pepper

2 cups milk
1½ tablespoons horse-radish
3 cups diced cooked potatoes
¼ cup grated Cheddar cheese

Melt butter; add flour, salt, mustard and pepper. Blend until smooth. Slowly add milk, stirring constantly. Cook until thickened; add horse-radish. Blend sauce with potatoes. Pour into greased 1½-quart casserole. Sprinkle with cheese.

Broccoli

1 package frozen broccoli
½ cup water
¼ teaspoon salt
2 tablespoons butter, melted

Place broccoli, water and salt in saucepan. Cover tightly. Before serving, drain and season with butter.

Apricot Cobbler

1½ cups cooked dried apricots
1 teaspoon grated orange rind
3 tablespoons granulated sugar
½ cup brown sugar
¼ cup melted butter
¾ cup apricot juice
2 tablespoons shortening
2 cups biscuit mix
2 tablespoons sugar
⅔ cup milk
1 egg, beaten

Arrange drained apricots, skin side down, in greased 9-inch-square baking pan. Add rind, sugars and butter to *hot* apricot juice and pour over apricots. Cut shortening into biscuit mix. Add sugar, milk and well-beaten egg. Drop dough on hot apricot mixture. Serve hot.

Baking Directions

Preheat oven to moderate, 375° F. Place creamed potatoes and broccoli on lower shelf. On shelf directly above, place cobbler and salmon. Bake everything 35 minutes.

Menu 13. Salmon and Potato Ring for Four

(45-MINUTE OVEN TIME)

SALMON AND POTATO RING   LEMON BUTTER SAUCE (MENU 5)
GREEN PEAS IN CREAM   PARSLEYED CAULIFLOWERETS
PART-BAKED PARKER HOUSE ROLLS *
HOT CUPCAKES WITH CHERRY SAUCE   COFFEE

*(Buy these.)

Salmon and Potato Ring

2 cups mashed potatoes
2 cups salmon, flaked
⅔ cup milk
2 tablespoons lemon juice
2 eggs, beaten

1 tablespoon onion juice
½ teaspoon salt
⅛ teaspoon pepper
¼ cup chopped stuffed olives

Blend potatoes, salmon, milk, lemon juice, eggs, onion juice, salt and pepper. Mix thoroughly. Fold in chopped olives. Pack into greased 1½-quart ring mold.

Green Peas in Cream

1 package frozen peas
¼ cup water
½ teaspoon sugar
2 tablespoons butter

1 tablespoon cream
¼ teaspoon salt
1/16 teaspoon pepper

Place peas in saucepan. Add water, sugar and butter. Cover tightly. Before serving season with cream, salt and pepper, and pile into center of salmon ring.

Parsleyed Cauliflowerets

1 small head cauliflower
½ cup milk
¼ cup water

½ teaspoon salt
2 tablespoon butter, melted
1 tablespoon chopped parsley

Soak cauliflower, head down, in water to cover to which salt has been added. Drain and separate into flowerets. Cut stem in half as far up as the flowers. Place in saucepan; add milk, water and salt. Cover tightly. Before serving drain, add butter and parsley.

Cupcakes

¼ cup shortening	1½ teaspoons baking powder
½ cup sugar	¼ teaspoon salt
1 egg	½ cup milk
1¼ cups sifted fluor	1 teaspoon vanilla

Cream shortening and sugar. Add egg and beat until fluffy. Sift together flour, baking powder and salt. Add alternately with milk and vanilla to creamed mixture. Pour into well-greased cupcake pans. Makes 8 large cupcakes. Spoon over with cherry sauce or sift over with confectioners' sugar and serve warm with ice cream.

CHERRY SAUCE

1 cup cherry juice	1 cup bing cherries
1¼ tablespoons cornstarch	1 tablespoon butter
¼ cup sugar	2 drops almond extract
¼ cup water	

Bring cherry juice to a boil. Combine cornstarch and sugar. Add water and pour into hot cherry juice. Bring to a boil, stirring constantly. Add cherries, butter and almond extract. Serve hot over cupcakes.

Baking Directions

Preheat oven to moderate, 350° F. Place peas and cauliflower on lower shelf in oven. On shelf directly above, place salmon ring and cupcakes. Bake 25 minutes. Remove cupcakes, add part baked rolls and bake 20 minutes longer. Total oven time 45 minutes.

Menu 14. Baked Salmon Steak for Four

(45-MINUTE OVEN TIME)

CHILLED FRESH FRUIT CUP

BAKED SALMON STEAK   CUCUMBER SAUCE

FROZEN PEAS   NEW POTATOES WITH PARSLEY BUTTER

DEEP-DISH SOUR CHERRY PIE   COFFEE

Baked Salmon Steak

¼ cup prepared French
dressing
¼ teaspoon salt
⅛ teaspoon pepper
½ onion, thinly sliced

½ lemon, thinly sliced
1 tablespoon onion juice
2 pounds fresh salmon steaks
1 tablespoon melted butter

Mix French dressing with salt, pepper, onion and lemon slices. Marinate salmon steaks in mixture in refrigerator for 1 hour, turning once. Place fish on sheet of aluminum foil in baking pan. Pour onion juice over it. Baste with melted butter and then with liquor in pan. Serve with cucumber sauce.

CUCUMBER SAUCE

¼ teaspoon salt
⅛ teaspoon cayenne pepper
½ pint heavy cream, whipped

1 medium-sized cucumber
2 tablespoons vinegar

Add salt and cayenne pepper to whipped cream. Pare, chop and drain cucumber; add vinegar. Slowly combine whipped cream and cucumber. Chill and serve.

Frozen Garden Peas

1 package frozen peas
¼ teaspoon sugar
½ cup water

2 tablespoons butter
¼ teaspoon salt
⅛ teaspoon pepper

Place frozen peas, sugar and water in saucepan. Cover tightly. Before serving, drain peas, and season with butter, salt and pepper.

New Potatoes with Parsley Butter

8 new potatoes
1½ cups hot water
½ teaspoon salt

3 tablespoons melted butter
3 tablespoons chopped parsley

Wash potatoes, using stiff brush. Place in saucepan. Add water and salt. Cover tightly. Serve *unpeeled* with melted butter and chopped parsley.

Deep-Dish Sour Cherry Pie

2 cups canned sour pitted
    cherries, drained
1 cup sugar
3 tablespoons flour

¼ teaspoon nutmeg
¼ cup canned cherry juice
2 tablespoons butter
1 package pastry mix

Reserve cherry juice. Combine sugar, flour and nutmeg. Add to cherry juice. Let stand until sugar is dissolved. Stir frequently. Arrange cherries in deep baking dish. Pour over juice; dot with butter. Prepare pastry and roll out to ⅛-inch thickness. Cut to fit top of dish, allowing ½ inch to turn over. Place over cherries. Crimp edges. Cut crust in four places to allow steam to escape.

Baking Directions

Preheat oven to hot, 450° F. Place peas and potatoes on lower shelf; on shelf directly above, place pie and salmon. After 15 minutes baking, reduce heat to moderate 350°. Baste salmon with liquid in pan and continue baking 30 minutes longer. Total oven time 45 minutes.

Menu 15. Salmon Loaf for Five
(50-MINUTE OVEN TIME)

TOMATO JUICE

SALMON LOAF

POTATOES EN CASSEROLE   FRENCH GREEN BEANS

CABBAGE FRUIT MOLD   BREAD AND BUTTER

WINE-BAKED APPLES   GINGER SNAPS *   TEA

* (Buy these.)

Salmon Loaf

2½ cups cooked flaked salmon

½ teaspoon salt

1 tablespoon onion juice

2 tablespoons lemon juice

½ cup cracker crumbs

3 tablespoons melted butter

½ cup scalded milk

3 egg yolks, beaten

3 egg whites, beaten stiff

4 hard-cooked eggs

Combine flaked salmon, salt, onion juice, lemon juice, crumbs, butter, milk and beaten egg yolks. Blend thoroughly and fold in beaten egg whites. Pour half of this mixture into greased loaf pan; arrange peeled, hard-cooked eggs down the center of pan and cover with remaining salmon mixture.

Potatoes en Casserole

5 medium-sized potatoes

¼ teaspoon salt

⅛ teaspoon pepper

4 tablespoons melted butter

Wash, peel and cut potatoes into ⅛-inch slices. Place potatoes in 1½-quart casserole with salt and pepper. Pour melted butter over and cover tightly.

French Green Beans

1 package frozen French-cut green beans

¼ cup water

2 tablespoons butter

1 tablespoon chopped pimento

1 tablespoon chopped chives

2 tablespoons fine bread crumbs

2 teaspoons melted butter

Place frozen beans, water, butter, pimento and chives in 1-quart casserole and cover tightly. Before serving, toss beans in mixture of bread crumbs and melted butter.

Wine-Baked Apples

5 medium-sized cooking apples
⅔ cup raisins
1¼ cups white wine

¼ teaspoon grated lemon rind
3 tablespoons sugar
1½ tablespoons butter

Wash and core apples. Soak raisins in wine for 30 minutes. Fill center of apples with soaked raisins, sprinkle with lemon rind and sugar. Dot apples with butter and pour balance of wine slowly over all. Bake in greased pan.

Baking Directions

Preheat oven to moderate, 375° F. Place potatoes and green beans on lower shelf; place salmon loaf and apples on shelf directly above. Bake 50 minutes.

Nice Addition: Cabbage Fruit Mold

½ cup seedless grapes
1 banana, sliced
1 cup melon balls
2 teaspoons lemon juice
2 cups shredded cabbage
¼ cup sliced stuffed olives

½ teaspoon salt
1 package lime gelatine
1 cup hot water
1 cup ice water
Lettuce leaves

Combine grapes, sliced banana, melon balls, lemon juice, cabbage, olives and salt, and chill in refrigerator. Dissolve gelatine in hot water, add ice water and chill until mixture begins to set. Fold in chilled mixed fruit, and chill until firm. Unmold on crisp lettuce leaves.

Menu 16. Swordfish Steaks for Four
(30-MINUTE OVEN TIME)

FISH STEAKS   PICKLE RELISH
MASHED POTATO BALLS   SCALLOPED FRESH TOMATOES
COLESLAW WITH SOUR CREAM (MENU 8)
GINGER PEARS   SPICE WAFERS *   TEA

*(Buy these.)

Fish Steaks

4 half-pound swordfish steaks	⅛ teaspoon pepper
1 egg	⅛ teaspoon marjoram
2 tablespoons milk	1½ cups crushed corn flakes
¼ teaspoon salt	2 tablespoons butter

Wipe fish steaks with damp cloth. Beat egg, milk, salt and pepper and marjoram together. Dip fish in egg; roll in corn flakes. Place in greased baking pan. Dot with butter.

Mashed Potato Balls

1 egg yolk	⅛ teaspoon pepper
1 teaspoon onion juice	2 cups cold mashed potatoes
¼ teaspoon salt	2 teaspoons butter

Beat egg yolk with onion juice, salt and pepper. Add mashed potato. Stir until well blended. Shape into 4 balls. Place in greased pan. Make a hollow in each ball. Place ½ teaspoon butter in each.

Scalloped Fresh Tomatoes

1 quart diced fresh tomatoes	2 cups crushed crackers
½ teaspoon salt	½ cup grated Cheddar cheese
¼ teaspoon pepper	3 tablespoons butter

Place layer of tomatoes in greased 1½-quart casserole; season with salt and pepper. Add a layer of crumbs and cheese. Dot with butter and repeat, having crumbs and cheese on top.

Ginger Pears

4 fresh pears	⅔ cup sugar
2 teaspoons grated lemon rind	1½ cups boiling water
3 tablespoons candied ginger, chopped	2 tablespoons lemon juice

Pare pears. Cut in half lengthwise. Remove core. Place in greased 8-inch baking dish; sprinkle with lemon rind and chopped ginger. Dissolve sugar in boiling water. Add lemon juice. Pour over pears. Cover tightly.

Baking Directions

Preheat oven to very hot, 475° F. Place potatoes and pears on lower shelf. On shelf directly above, place tomatoes and fish steaks. Bake 30 minutes.

Menu 17. Tri-Fish Pie for Six

(35-MINUTE OVEN TIME)

TRI-FISH PIE

WHIPPED POTATOES   SLICED CARROTS

TOSSED SALAD WITH ROQUEFORT DRESSING (MENU 54)

LEMON TARTLETS   COFFEE

Tri-Fish Pie

1 quart boiling water
1 onion, peeled
1 carrot
1 stalk celery
1 teaspoon salt
¼ teaspoon pepper
1½ pounds haddock
1 pint bay scallops
½ pound shrimp

2 tablespoons butter
1 tablespoon finely chopped
  onion
2 tablespoons flour
1 can condensed cream-of-
  chicken soup
1½ teaspoons chopped parsley
1 package pastry mix
1 tablespoon cream

Into the boiling water put onion and carrot. Add whole celery stalk, salt and pepper. Boil 10 minutes. Add haddock in 1 piece and cook, *covered,* until tender, about 15 minutes. Remove fish to platter. Place scallops and shelled-and-veined shrimp in liquid. Cover and simmer until tender. Remove skin and bones from cooked halibut. Do not throw skin and bones away. Remove scallops and shrimp from liquid. Add skin and bones to liquid and simmer 15 minutes. Strain out vegetables and fish bones, and save fish stock.

Melt butter; add chopped onion and cook slowly until onion is tender but not browned. Add flour and stir until smooth. Pour in slowly 2 cups of the strained fish stock; add chicken soup and blend. Add parsley. Break fish into large flakes. Place in greased 2½-quart casserole alternate layers of fish, scallops and shrimp.

Pour sauce over all. Cover with rolled-out pastry. Flute pastry
to casserole edge. Brush with cream. Cut steam vents in pastry.

Whipped Potatoes

6 medium-sized potatoes	1/8 teaspoon pepper
1/4 cup water	2 tablespoons butter
1/4 teaspoon salt	3 tablespoons hot milk

Peel and thinly slice potatoes. Place in saucepan with water and
salt. Cover tightly. Before serving mash and season with pepper,
butter and milk.

Sliced Carrots

8 small carrots	1/4 cup water
1/4 teaspoon salt	1/8 teaspoon pepper
1/4 teaspoon sugar	2 tablespoons butter

Scrape and thinly slice carrots. Place in saucepan with salt, sugar
and water. Cover tightly. Before serving season with pepper and
butter.

Lemon Tartlets

2 cups crushed corn flakes	1/3 cup lemon juice
1/3 cup melted butter	1 1/2 cups sugar
1/3 cup sugar	2 eggs, beaten
1/2 teaspoon grated lemon rind	1 1/4 cups spongecake crumbs

Mix together corn flakes, butter and sugar, and line 6 greased
custard cups. Combine lemon rind, juice, sugar, eggs and cake
crumbs. Beat until smooth. Pour into crumb-lined custard cups.

Baking Directions

Preheat oven to very hot, 450° F. Place tarts and potatoes on
lower shelf. On shelf directly above, place fish and carrots. After
10 minutes baking time, reduce heat to moderate, 350° F., and
bake 25 minutes longer. Total baking time 35 minutes.

Menu 18. Tuna Pie for Six

(30-MINUTE OVEN TIME)

TUNA PIE   MUSTARD PICKLE

CARROT CURLS AND SCALLIONS

BUTTERED BROCCOLI

HOT CRISPY ROLLS *   BUTTER

BANANA CAKE WITH WHIPPED CREAM   COFFEE

* (Buy these.)

Tuna Fish Pie

3 cups crushed potato chips
2 seven-ounce cans white tuna
    fish
½ cup black olives
5 hard-cooked eggs
¼ cup butter

¼ cup flour
¼ teaspoon salt
⅛ teaspoon pepper
¼ teaspoon dry mustard
1½ cups milk

Grease 2-quart casserole and line with 2 cups crushed potato chips. Drain off tuna oil and save. Flake tuna fish. Slice olives from pits. Peel and slice eggs. Melt butter; add flour, salt, pepper and mustard, and stir until smooth. Slowly add milk and fish oil. Cook, stirring constantly, until smooth and thickened. Add tuna fish, olives and sliced eggs. Pour into potato-chip-lined casserole. Top with remaining potato chips.

Buttered Broccoli

2 packages frozen broccoli
½ cup boiling water
2 tablespoons butter
¼ teaspoon salt

⅛ teaspoon pepper
2 tablespoons grated Cheddar
    cheese

Thaw broccoli and place in saucepan with water; cover tightly. Before serving, drain and season with butter, salt and pepper. Sprinkle with grated cheese.

Banana Cake

2¼ cups sifted cake flour	1 cup sugar
2½ teaspoons baking powder	2 eggs
½ teaspoon baking soda	1 teaspoon vanilla
½ teaspoon salt	1 cup mashed ripe bananas
½ cup shortening	¼ cup buttermilk

Sift together flour, baking powder, soda and salt. Cream shortening; add sugar gradually and continue creaming until fluffy. Add eggs, one at a time, beating well after each addition. Stir in vanilla. Add sifted flour mixture alternately with bananas and milk. Turn into 2 greased 9-inch layer-cake pans.

WHIPPED-CREAM TOPPING

¾ cup heavy cream	1 banana, sliced
2 tablespoons sugar	2 cake layers
½ teaspoon vanilla	

Whip cream, sugar and vanilla until stiff. Spread half on lower layer of cake; top with banana. Place second cake layer on top and cover with remaining sweetened whipped cream.

Baking Directions

Preheat oven to moderate, 375° F. Place tuna fish and broccoli on lower shelf; on shelf directly above, place cake. Bake 25 minutes. Remove cake. Place rolls on top shelf and bake 5 minutes longer. Total oven time 30 minutes.

Menu 19. Barbecued Chicken for Four
(60-MINUTE OVEN TIME)

CHILLED TOMATO JUICE

BARBECUED CHICKEN

BAKED ACORN SQUASH   PEAS AND CARROTS

CABBAGE FRUIT MOLD (MENU 15)

PEANUT-BUTTER BREAD   BUTTER   TEA

Barbecued Chicken

2½-pound chicken, cut in serving pieces
4 tablespoons shortening
1 large onion, sliced
3 tablespoons vinegar
3 tablespoons brown sugar
¼ cup lemon juice
1 cup tomato catsup
3 tablespoons Worcestershire sauce
1 tablespoon prepared mustard
1¼ cups water
½ cup diced celery
½ teaspoon salt
¼ teaspoon pepper

Brown chicken in shortening and place in 3-quart greased casserole. Blend remaining ingredients with fat in skillet, bring to a boil and pour over browned chicken in casserole.

Baked Acorn Squash

2 acorn squash
½ teaspoon salt
¼ teaspoon pepper
4 teaspoons butter

Wash squash; cut in half and remove seeds and stringy pulp. Place squash, cut-side up, in casserole that is just large enough to hold halves upright. Sprinkle each piece with salt and pepper and place a teaspoon of butter in each cavity. Pour warm water around squash to the depth of 1 inch. Cover tightly; aluminum foil or waxed paper may be used.

Peas and Carrots

3 tablespoons butter
2 tablespoons water

1 package frozen peas and carrots

Place butter, water and frozen peas and carrots into 1-quart casserole dish and cover tightly.

Peanut-Butter Bread

½ cup peanut butter
1 tablespoon shortening
⅓ cup sugar
1 egg, beaten
2 cups sifted all-purpose flour

2½ teaspoons baking powder
½ teaspoon salt
1¼ cups milk
1 teaspoon vanilla
½ cup chopped dates

Cream together peanut butter, shortening and sugar; add egg and blend thoroughly. Sift dry ingredients together and add alternately with milk. Fold in vanilla and dates, and pour into well-greased loaf pan.

Baking Directions

Preheat oven to moderate, 350° F. Place squash on lower shelf, and chicken and peanut-butter bread on shelf directly above. At the end of 30 minutes, place peas and carrots on shelf with squash; continue baking 30 minutes longer. Total baking time 60 minutes.

Menu 20. Deviled Chicken for Four
(60-MINUTE OVEN TIME)

DEVILED.CHICKEN

BAKED SPINACH   BAKED FRENCH FRIED POTATOES

HOT POPPYSEED ROLLS *   BUTTER

STRAWBERRY CUSTARD   TEA

*(Buy these.)

Deviled Chicken

2½-pound chicken, cut into
    serving pieces
¼ cup melted butter
1 teaspoon prepared mustard
1 teaspoon vinegar
1 teaspoon paprika

¼ teaspoon salt
⅛ teaspoon pepper
1 tablespoon finely-chopped
    onion
1 cup soft bread crumbs
2 tablespoons melted butter

Place chicken in 15-by 9-inch baking pan and pour over ¼ cup melted butter. Combine the mustard, vinegar, paprika, salt, pepper and chopped onion, and spread on chicken. Blend the soft bread crumbs and 2 tablespoons of melted butter, and sprinkle over all.

Baked Spinach

2 pounds spinach
¼ cup flour
1 cup milk
¼ cup melted butter

½ teaspoon salt
¾ cup fine bread crumbs
¼ cup grated Cheddar cheese

Wash spinach thoroughly and chop coarsely. Divide in half; place half in bottom of 15-by 9-inch, greased baking pan, sprinkle with flour and add remaining spinach. Combine the milk, melted butter and salt, and pour over the spinach. Blend the bread crumbs and grated cheese and sprinkle over all.

Baked French Fried Potatoes

6 white potatoes	2 teaspoons salt
6 tablespoons melted butter	

Pare potatoes and cut into strips about ½-inch wide and ¼-inch thick. Arrange potato strips in baking pan so that they do not overlap. Pour the melted butter over them and sprinkle with salt.

Strawberry Custard

1 cup frozen strawberries, partially drained	3 tablespoons sugar
	½ teaspoon nutmeg
2 eggs, beaten	1 teaspoon vanilla
2 cups milk	2 cups stale cake cubes

Grease 4 large or 6 small custard cups. Divide strawberries equally among custard cups. Combine beaten eggs, milk, sugar, nutmeg, vanilla and cake cubes; blend well and pour carefully over strawberries. Place custard cups in pan of water and bake.

Baking Directions

Preheat oven to moderate, 350° F. Place chicken and spinach on lower shelf. On shelf directly above place custard and potatoes. Bake everything 1 hour. Add rolls to heat last 10 minutes. *Note:* Stir potatoes once during baking time.

Menu 21. Chicken Italian-Style for Four
(60-MINUTE OVEN TIME)

CHICKEN ITALIAN-STYLE
STEAMED POTATOES AND TURNIPS   STEAMED BROCCOLI .
ITALIAN BREAD *   BUTTER
SPUMONI   MACAROONS *   COFFEE
(BREAKFAST CROWN CAKE FOR TOMORROW)
*(Buy these.)

Chicken Italian-Style

2-pound chicken, cut in serving
   pieces
¼ cup shortening, melted
2 teaspoons chopped parsley
½ cup diced celery
1 teaspoon salt

¼ teaspoon pepper
⅛ teaspoon garlic salt
2 bay leaves
½ cup dry white wine
¼ cup water

Brown chicken on both sides in melted shortening in frying pan on top of stove, add remaining ingredients, cover tightly and place in oven.

Steamed Potatoes and Turnips

1 small turnip
3 potatoes
1 cup water

½ teaspoon salt
½ teaspoon sugar

Pare turnip and potatoes, cut in 1-inch cubes and place in 2-quart casserole dish with remaining ingredients; cover tightly.

Steamed Broccoli

½ cup water
½ teaspoon salt

1 package frozen broccoli

Place water, salt and frozen broccoli in 1-quart casserole dish; cover tightly.

Breakfast Crown Cake

¼ cup warm water
¼ teaspoon sugar
1 package granular yeast
1 cup milk, scalded
⅓ cup shortening
¼ cup sugar
½ teaspoon salt
2 eggs, beaten
4 cups sifted all-purpose flour

½ cup butter, melted
¾ cup sugar
½ teaspoon cinnamon
½ cup finely-chopped nuts
1 cup chopped candied fruits
1 cup sifted confectioners sugar
3 tablespoons milk
½ teaspoon vanilla

Blend water and ¼ teaspoon sugar; sprinkle yeast gently over this mixture and set aside. Combine scalded milk, shortening, ¼ cup sugar and salt; stir together until all ingredients have melted. Blend milk and yeast mixtures and add beaten eggs and 2 cups of the sifted flour. Beat well, add remaining flour and continue beating about 2 minutes. Turn dough out on lightly-floured cloth and knead well. Place kneaded dough in large greased bowl, cover and set in warm place until double in size.

Turn raised dough out on floured cloth, roll to ½-inch thickness, cut in ½-inch cubes and shape into balls. Roll these balls in the melted butter, then in combined mixture of ¾ cup sugar and cinnamon and lastly in finely-chopped nuts. Place a layer of these balls in greased 9-inch tube pan, sprinkle with some of the candied fruit; proceed the same way until all the dough and fruit are used. Cover and let rise about 1½ hours.

Uncover and bake. When cake is baked, allow to cool 5 minutes; then loosen at sides and remove cake from pan and place on rack. Combine the sifted confectioners sugar, milk and vanilla; blend well and pour over cake.

Baking Directions

Preheat oven to moderate, 350° F. Place chicken on lower shelf; at the end of 20 minutes, set potatoes and turnips on shelf with chicken and place crown cake and broccoli on shelf directly above. Continue baking 40 minutes longer. Total baking time 60 minutes.

Menu 22. Oven-Fried Chicken for Four
(60-MINUTE OVEN TIME)

OVEN-FRIED CHICKEN

BAKED WHITE POTATOES   STRING BEAN SPECIAL

TOSSED SALAD WITH ROQUEFORT DRESSING (MENU 54)

ORANGE CUPCAKES WITH ORANGE FROSTING   TEA

Oven-Fried Chicken

2-pound chicken, cut in serving   1 teaspoon salt
   pieces   ¼ teaspoon pepper
½ cup all-purpose flour   ¼ cup melted shortening

Dredge chicken in mixture of flour, salt and pepper. Pour melted shortening into 9-by 15-inch baking pan, add chicken, skin-side down, and sprinkle with any flour mixture that is left. Cover baking pan with a cooky sheet or a piece of aluminum foil, but do not secure foil tightly around pan.

Baked White Potatoes

4 medium-sized white potatoes   1 teaspoon shortening

Scrub potatoes well, dry and rub with shortening. Cut a cross on top of each potato to prevent bursting in oven.

String Bean Special

1 small onion, chopped fine   ⅛ teaspoon pepper
2 tablespoons salad oil   1 package frozen string beans,
¼ cup chili sauce   thawed
1 teaspoon salt

Simmer onion in salad oil until tender but not browned. Add remaining ingredients, blend well and pour into greased 1-quart casserole dish; cover tightly.

Orange Cupcakes

2¼ cups sifted cake flour
3½ teaspoons baking powder
1 teaspoon salt
1½ cups sugar
½ cup melted shortening

¾ cup milk
2 tablespoons orange concentrate
2 eggs

Sift together flour, baking powder, salt and sugar; add melted shortening and milk. Beat well and add orange concentrate and eggs; continue beating thoroughly. Fill 10 large, greased muffin pans or 16 small muffin pans, half full. When baked, cover with orange frosting.

ORANGE FROSTING

2 egg whites, slightly beaten
1 tablespoon orange concentrate

Sifted confectioners sugar

Combine egg whites and orange concentrate; add enough confectioners sugar to make the consistency you desire for spreading.

Baking Directions

Preheat oven to moderate, 350° F. Place covered chicken and potatoes on lower shelf; cupcakes directly above. At the end of 35 minutes, remove cupcakes and take cover from chicken. Place string beans on upper shelf and continue baking 25 minutes longer. Total oven time 60 minutes.

Menu 23. Roast Chicken for Four
(2-HOUR OVEN TIME)

CHILLED TOMATO JUICE   CELERY AND OLIVES
ROAST STUFFED CHICKEN   CURRANT JELLY
WHIPPED POTATOES   SPINACH WITH EGG GARNISH
POUND CAKE   CHOCOLATE ICE CREAM   COFFEE

Roast Stuffed Chicken

5-pound roasting chicken
2½ cups stale bread cubes
1 teaspoon sage
2 tablespoons finely-chopped
    onion
2 tablespoons butter

½ teaspoon salt
¼ teaspoon pepper
⅓ cup boiling water
1 teaspoon salt
3 tablespoons butter
2 tablespoons flour

Remove pinfeathers, singe and wash chicken. Be sure oil sac is cut off and lungs removed.

Combine bread cubes and sage. Simmer onions in 2 tablespoons butter until tender, add bread mixture, ½ teaspoon salt, pepper and water. Blend well and stuff chicken. Combine 1 teaspoon salt, 3 tablespoons butter, and flour, and rub on surface of chicken. Place chicken, breast side up, on rack in shallow baking pan.

Whipped Potatoes

5 medium-sized potatoes
½ teaspoon salt
½ cup water

2 tablespoons butter
⅛ teaspoon pepper
3 tablespoons hot milk

Wash potatoes, pare and cut in quarters. Place in 1½-quart casserole with salt and water; cover tightly and place in oven. When baked, mash with remaining ingredients and whip until fluffy.

Spinach with Egg Garnish

2 packages frozen spinach
¼ cup water
2 tablespoons butter

¼ teaspoon salt
⅛ teaspoon pepper
1 hard-cooked egg

Place frozen spinach in 1-quart casserole with water and cover tightly. Before serving, drain spinach thoroughly; chop and add butter, salt and pepper. Garnish with sliced, hard-cooked egg.

Pound Cake

1 cup butter
1 cup sugar
4 eggs

2 cups sifted cake flour
½ teaspoon baking powder
1 teaspoon vanilla

Cream butter, add sugar gradually and cream thoroughly. Add eggs, one at a time, beating well after each addition. Sift flour and baking powder together and stir into first mixture with vanilla. Beat ten hard strokes; pour into greased loaf pan.

Baking Directions

Preheat oven to moderate, 325° F. Place chicken on lower shelf; place cake on shelf directly above. At the end of 50 minutes, remove cake and continue baking chicken for 40 minutes. Then place potatoes and spinach on upper shelf and bake 30 minutes longer. Total baking time 2 hours.

Menu 24. Spanish Chicken Stew for Six

(90-MINUTE OVEN TIME)

SPANISH CHICKEN STEW

SCALLOPED CORN   FROZEN VEGETABLE SALAD

HOT YEAST ROLLS   BUTTER

CUSTARD CAKE PUDDING   TEA

Spanish Chicken Stew

4-pound chicken, cut in serving
  pieces
¼ cup olive oil
1 large Spanish onion, sliced
1 cup canned tomatoes
1 small clove garlic, chopped
  fine
¾ cup peas, canned or leftover

¾ cup corn, canned or leftover
1 cup raw rice
½ teaspoon chili powder
1½ teaspoons salt
⅟₁₆ teaspoon red pepper
⅛ teaspoon black pepper
2 cups stock

Wipe chicken pieces with damp cloth and place skin-side up in
2½-quart, greased casserole dish. Combine remaining ingredients
in order given, blend well and pour over chicken; cover tightly.

Scalloped Corn

2 eggs
½ cup milk
¼ teaspoon salt
⅛ teaspoon pepper
1 teaspoon onion juice

2½ cups (No. 2 can) creamed-
  style corn
⅔ cup soft bread crumbs
2 tablespoons melted butter

Beat the eggs and milk together; add salt, pepper and onion
juice, and blend well. Stir in the corn and pour mixture into a
greased loaf pan. Top with bread crumbs which have been
tossed in melted butter.

Hot Yeast Rolls

1 package granular yeast
¼ cup lukewarm water
1 cup milk, scalded
2 tablespoons shortening,
  melted

2 tablespoons sugar
1 teaspoon salt
1 egg, well beaten
3½ cups sifted all-purpose flour

Sprinkle yeast slowly over lukewarm water. Combine milk, shortening, sugar and salt, and blend thoroughly; cool to luke-warm; add yeast mixture and well-beaten egg. Stir in flour, one cup at a time, beating well after each addition. Place dough in large, greased mixing bowl, cover with towel and let stand in warm place to double in size—about 1½ to 2 hours.

Turn out on floured board or pastry cloth and roll out about ½ inch thick. Cut with 2-inch cooky cutter and place on greased cooky sheets about 2 inches apart; cover and let stand in warm place for about 1 hour to rise. This recipe makes approximately 2 dozen rolls.

Custard Cake Pudding

2 cups cake cubes	½ teaspoon salt
1 quart milk, scalded	1 teaspoon vanilla
2 eggs	¼ teaspoon nutmeg
¼ cup sugar	3 tablespoons melted butter

Combine cake cubes and milk; beat eggs slightly with sugar and salt, and gradually stir in milk mixture. Add vanilla, nutmeg and melted butter, and blend well; pour into greased loaf pan.

Baking Directions

Preheat oven to moderate, 350° F. Place chicken at rear of lower shelf. At the end of 45 minutes baking time, set corn and cake pudding on shelf with chicken; place rolls on shelf directly above. Continue baking 45 minutes longer. Total baking time 90 minutes.

Salad Suggestion: Frozen Vegetable Salad

1 cup shredded cabbage	1 tablespoon finely-chopped
1 cup diced celery	onion
½ cup grated, raw carrot	½ teaspoon salt
¼ cup finely-chopped green	⅛ teaspoon pepper
pepper	⅔ cup mayonnaise
	½ cup heavy cream, whipped

Combine cabbage, celery, carrot, green pepper, onion, salt and pepper. Stir in mayonnaise and mix thoroughly. Fold in whipped cream; pour into ice-cube tray and freeze until firm. Serve on crisp lettuce leaves.

Menu 25. Rolled Chicken Livers for Six

(20-MINUTE OVEN TIME)

ROLLED CHICKEN LIVERS

BAKED MACARONI AND CHEESE

PINEAPPLE COLESLAW

STRAWBERRY CREAM-CHEESE TARTS   COFFEE

Rolled Chicken Livers

1½ pounds chicken livers
4 tablespoons prepared mustard
4 tablespoons finely-chopped
   olives

½ pound bacon
½ cup fine bread crumbs

Cut each chicken liver in half and coat with combined mixture of mustard and chopped olives. Cut bacon strips in half and wrap around each piece of liver. Roll in bread crumbs and place in greased 9-by 12-inch baking pan.

Baked Macaroni and Cheese

8 ounces (1 package) raw
   macaroni
1 quart boiling water
1 tablespoon salt
3 tablespoons butter
3 tablespoons flour
½ teaspoon salt

¼ teaspoon pepper
2 cups milk
⅔ cup grated American cheese
½ cup fine bread crumbs
¼ cup grated American cheese
1 tablespoon melted butter

Cook macaroni in boiling water with 1 tablespoon salt until tender; drain in cold water. Melt the 3 tablespoons butter in saucepan; stir in flour, salt and pepper. Slowly add milk, stirring constantly, and cook until thickened. Remove from heat and stir in the ⅔ cup grated cheese. Place drained macaroni in greased 2-quart casserole; pour over cheese sauce. Blend together bread crumbs, ¼ cup grated cheese and melted butter. Sprinkle over macaroni and cheese.

Strawberry Cream-Cheese Tarts

2½ cups sifted all-purpose flour	¾ cup shortening
1 teaspoon salt	4 to 5 tablespoons cold water

Sift flour with salt and cut in half of the shortening until it looks like cornmeal; cut in remaining shortening until all particles are about the size of navy beans. Add enough water gradually to make a firm dough and mix lightly with a fork. Roll dough on floured pastry cloth to about ⅛-inch thickness. Cut into six 5-inch rounds and fit them over muffin pans or custard cups, pressing firmly to hold shape. If using custard cups, arrange them on a cooky sheet before setting in oven. Allow baked tart shells to cool before filling.

FILLING

¼ pound cream cheese	2 cups sliced strawberries
⅓ cup heavy cream	½ cup sugar
1 tablespoon sugar	6 whole strawberries

Soften cream cheese, add cream and beat, while gradually adding 1 tablespoon sugar. Line tart shells generously with this mixture. Combine sliced strawberries with remaining sugar and fill shells. Garnish with whole strawberries.

Baking Directions

Preheat oven to hot, 425° F. Place chicken livers on lower shelf and macaroni and tart shells on shelf directly above. Bake everything 20 minutes.

Good Extra: Pineapple Coleslaw

3 cups shredded cabbage	⅔ cup heavy cream
1 cup crushed pineapple, drained	¼ cup vinegar
2 celery stalks, finely diced	⅓ teaspoon salt
1 small green pepper, chopped	¼ teaspoon pepper
	⅛ teaspoon dry mustard

Combine shredded cabbage with pineapple, celery and green pepper, and mix well. Beat cream until stiff, gradually adding remaining ingredients. Fold cream mixture into combined vegetables. Chill and serve.

Menu 26. Duck Dinner for Four
(2½-HOUR OVEN TIME)

ROAST DUCK   BROWN RICE DRESSING

LETTUCE HEARTS AND CHILI SAUCE DRESSING (MENU 50)

TINY GREEN PEAS

SPOON BREAD   BUTTER   APPLE SAUCE *

CHILLED SPICED PEARS   MOLASSES COOKIES *   COFFEE

*(Buy these.)

Roast Duck

5-pound duck   ¼ teaspoon salt
2 tablespoons lemon juice

Cut off wing tips. Remove pinfeathers and singe. Wash thoroughly inside and outside. Dry. Place lemon juice in cavity of bird and turn so that inside is well coated with juice. Sprinkle with salt. Fill with brown rice dressing.

BROWN RICE DRESSING

1 cup cooked brown rice   ¼ teaspoon salt
1 cup mashed potatoes   ⅛ teaspoon pepper
1 medium-sized onion, diced   ½ teaspoon crushed sage

Mix together rice, potatoes, onion, salt, pepper and sage. Fill duck cavity. Place, breast-side up, on rack in baking pan. Do not prick skin. Do not cover.

Tiny Green Peas

1 can tiny green peas   ¼ teaspoon salt
2 tablespoons butter   ⅛ teaspoon pepper
1 tablespoon water

Place drained peas in saucepan; add butter, water, salt and pepper. Cover tightly.

Spoon Bread

1 teaspoon salt	1 tablespoon sugar
2 cups boiling water	2 tablespoons butter
1 cup white corn meal	2 eggs, well beaten
1 cup cold milk	2 tablespoons butter

Add salt to boiling water. Stir in corn meal. Cook 5 minutes, stirring constantly. Add cold milk, sugar, butter and eggs. Pour into greased loaf pan. Serve on platter around duck. Dot with butter.

Baking Directions

Preheat oven to moderate, 325° F. Place duck on lower shelf; at the end of 1½ hours, place spoon bread on shelf directly above. Continue baking 45 minutes longer. Then set peas on shelf with spoon bread. Bake 15 minutes longer. Total oven time 2½ hours.

Light Dessert: Chilled Spiced Pears

2½ cups (No. 2 can) pears	¼ cup red cinnamon candies
3-inch stick cinnamon	½ pint heavy cream, whipped
3 whole cloves	(optional)

Drain pears and reserve juice. Add cinnamon, cloves and red candies to juice and boil 3 minutes. Arrange pears, curved side down, in round 9-inch pan. Pour over hot spiced juice. Before serving, remove cinnamon stick and cloves. Chill thoroughly. Serve in sherbet glasses. Top with whipped cream if desired.

Menu 27. Roast Goose for Six

(4½-HOUR OVEN TIME)

ROAST GOOSE WITH PRUNE AND APPLE STUFFING
GREEN CABBAGE AND RICE
ORANGE-AND-ONION SALAD
HOT WHOLE-WHEAT ROLLS * BUTTER
CHILLED MELON WITH LEMON WEDGE TEA
(CREAMY RICE PUDDING FOR TOMORROW)

*(Buy these.)

Roast Goose

12-pound goose
1 teaspoon salt
7 cups dry bread cubes
½ teaspoon salt
⅛ teaspoon pepper
1½ tablespoons chopped
  parsley
¼ cup chopped onion

3 cups tart apples, pared and
  diced fine
2 cups prunes, soaked overnight
½ cup pecans
2 eggs, beaten
2 cups boiling water

Singe goose and remove pinfeathers, lungs and oil sac from tail. Wash thoroughly inside and out. Use stiff brush on skin. Wipe dry. Rub inside and outer skin with 1 teaspoon salt. Blend together bread cubes, salt, pepper, parsley, onion, apples, prunes, pecans and eggs. Toss lightly. Stuff cavity of goose. Insert skewers and lace cord around them to close opening. Place breast-side up on a rack in a covered roasting pan. Prick skin around legs and wings to allow fat to run out; add water and cover. Remove cover during last 1¼ hours of roasting time.

Green Cabbage and Rice

6 cups green cabbage
3 cups cooked rice
¾ cup chopped onion
¾ cup diced green pepper

3 tablespoons bacon fat
1 teaspoon salt
2½ cups (No. 2 can) tomatoes

Place cabbage and rice in alternate layers in greased baking pan. Brown onion and green pepper in bacon fat. Add with salt to tomatoes, and pour over rice and cabbage.

Creamy Rice Pudding

3 tablespoons rice
1 tablespoon sugar
1 quart milk

½ teaspoon salt
½ teaspoon nutmeg
½ cup raisins (optional)

Wash rice under running water. Combine all ingredients. Pour into greased 9- by 12-inch baking pan. Stir 3 times during baking time.

Baking Directions

Preheat oven to moderate, 325° F. Place goose on lower shelf. Place rice pudding on shelf directly above. Bake 2¼ hours. Remove rice pudding. Bake 1 hour more and remove cover from goose. Place cabbage and rice on shelf directly above, and continue baking 1¼ hours longer. Add rolls to heat the last 10 minutes of oven time. Total oven time 4½ hours.

Tasty Extra: Orange-and-Onion Salad

3 California oranges
1 Bermuda onion, sliced

1 bunch water cress
½ cup French dressing

Peel oranges with sharp knife, being sure to remove all of white membrane. Remove orange sections, discarding membrane between. Arrange orange and onion on bed of chilled water cress. Pour over French dressing, and serve.

Menu 28. Prime Ribs of Beef for Four
(90-MINUTE OVEN TIME)

ROAST PRIME RIBS OF BEEF   YORKSHIRE PUDDING

STEAMED MASHED POTATOES   CARROTS IN CREAM

BUTTERED WHITE ONIONS

PINEAPPLE COLESLAW (MENU 25)

RASPBERRY SHERBET   LADY FINGERS *   COFFEE

*(Buy these.)

Roast Prime Ribs of Beef

3-pound standing rib roast of
    beef
1½ teaspoons salt

¼ teaspoon pepper
1 tablespoon flour

Wipe beef with damp cloth. Blend remaining ingredients and rub well into beef. Place fat side up in close-fitting baking pan.

Yorkshire Pudding

1 cup sifted all-purpose flour
¼ teaspoon salt
3 eggs, beaten

1 cup milk
8 teaspoons hot fat drippings

Sift flour and salt together; combine beaten eggs and milk. Blend flour and egg mixtures and beat vigorously for 3 minutes. Grease 8 muffin pans; place 1 teaspoon hot fat drippings from roast in each muffin cup and pour in batter.

Steamed Mashed Potatoes

8 medium-sized potatoes
½ cup water
2 tablespoons butter

¼ cup milk
¼ teaspoon salt
⅛ teaspoon pepper

Pare potatoes and cut in ¼-inch slices. Place in 2-quart casserole with water and cover tightly. Before serving, mash potatoes with remaining ingredients.

Carrots in Cream

6 medium-sized carrots	2 tablespoons cream
½ cup water	¼ teaspoon salt
2 tablespoons butter	⅟₁₆ teaspoon pepper

Wash, scrape and cut carrots in ⅛-inch slices. Place in 1-quart casserole and add water; cover tightly. Before serving, drain and season with remaining ingredients.

Buttered White Onions

12 small white onions	⅛ teaspoon pepper
½ cup water	2 tablespoons melted butter
½ teaspoon salt	

Peel onions and place in 1½-quart casserole with water, salt and pepper; cover tightly. Before serving, drain and toss onions in melted butter.

Baking Directions

Preheat oven to moderate, 325° F. Place beef on lower shelf and onions on shelf directly above. At the end of 45 minutes, set Yorkshire pudding on shelf with roast and place potatoes and carrots on shelf directly above. Increase oven temperature to hot, 400° F., and continue baking 45 minutes longer. Total baking time 90 minutes.

Menu 29. Sirloin Roast for Six
(75-MINUTE OVEN TIME)

SIRLOIN ROAST OF BEEF   BROWN GRAVY
CELERY AND OLIVES
BROWNED POTATOES   PARSLEY BUTTERED ONIONS
RHUBARB BETTY WITH ORANGE HARD SAUCE   COFFEE

Sirloin Roast of Beef

3-pound sirloin roast
2 teaspoons salt

½ teaspoon pepper
1 tablespoon butter

Wipe meat with damp cloth. Place on waxed paper. Rub with salt and pepper. Place in shallow baking pan. Dot with butter and sprinkle with any remaining salt and pepper. *Do not add any water.*

Browned Potatoes

6 medium-sized potatoes
1 cup boiling water
2 tablespoons melted butter

½ teaspoon salt
¼ teaspoon pepper

Wash and pare potatoes. Place in saucepan with boiling water. Cover and steam for 10 minutes. Drain. Brush with butter. Sprinkle with salt and pepper. Place around roast beef.

Parsley Buttered Onions

12 small white onions
½ cup water
1 tablespoon butter

¼ teaspoon salt
⅛ teaspoon pepper
1 tablespoon chopped parsley

Peel onions. Place in saucepan with water, butter, salt and pepper. Cover tightly. Before serving, toss with parsley.

Rhubarb Betty

½ cup butter
1 quart soft bread crumbs
2 pounds (about 4 cups) un-
cooked rhubarb, cut in
1½-inch pieces

1¾ cups sugar
½ teaspoon cinnamon
1 lemon, grated rind and juice
⅔ cup water

Melt butter and add crumbs. Toss until crumbs absorb all of the butter. Into buttered shallow 9-by 12-inch pan place a layer of rhubarb, then a layer of crumbs. Mix cinnamon with sugar and sprinkle a third of it over crumbs. Repeat, making 3 layers. Add lemon juice and rind to water and pour over rhubarb mixture.

ORANGE HARD SAUCE

⅓ cup butter
1¼ cups confectioners sugar

1 tablespoon orange concentrate

Cream butter. Add sugar gradually, beating well. Add orange concentrate and blend thoroughly. Chill before serving.

Baking Directions

Preheat oven to moderate, 375° F. Place beef and onions on lower shelf. On shelf directly above, place pudding. After 20 minutes, arrange potatoes around the roast. Bake 55 minutes longer. Total oven time 75 minutes.

Menu 30. Spiced Pot Roast Dinner for Six

(3-HOUR OVEN TIME)

CRANBERRY JUICE   CELERY AND RADISHES
SPICED POT ROAST
BAKED POTATOES   BUTTERNUT SQUASH
BAKED PEACH HALVES   GINGER SNAPS *   COFFEE

*(Buy these.)

Spiced Pot Roast

4-pound rump pot roast	1 large onion, sliced thin
½ cup flour	2 cups hot water
1 teaspoon salt	½ cup vinegar
¼ teaspoon pepper	1 bay leaf
3 tablespoons fat	1 teaspoon salt
5 whole cloves	

Rub meat well with mixture of flour, 1 teaspoon salt, and pepper. Melt fat in roasting pan on top of the range, and brown meat on all sides. Stick with whole cloves and top with onion slices. Combine water, vinegar, bay leaf and remaining salt; pour over roast and cover tightly.

Butternut Squash

1 large-sized butternut squash	2 tablespoons butter
½ teaspoon salt	½ teaspoon onion juice
¼ teaspoon pepper	

Wash and dry squash and put in pan in oven. At the end of baking time, cut squash in half and remove seeds and fibers. Scrape out tender pulp and mash with salt, pepper, butter and onion juice. Place in top of double boiler to keep warm.

Baked White Potatoes

6 baking potatoes	1 tablespoon shortening

Wash and dry potatoes; grease well with shortening. Prick each potato with fork to prevent bursting in oven.

Baked Peach Halves

3½ cups (No. 2½ can) peach halves, drained
4 large graham crackers, crushed
2 tablespoons melted butter
Juice ½ lemon

¼ teaspoon cinnamon
¼ teaspoon ground cloves
2 egg whites
2 tablespoons water
½ teaspoon vanilla
4 tablespoons sugar

Place drained peach halves, cut side up, in greased 9-inch shallow baking pan. Combine crushed graham crackers, melted butter, lemon juice, cinnamon and cloves; blend well and fill peach halves with this mixture. Beat egg whites with water until partially stiff; gradually add vanilla and sugar and continue to beat until stiff but not dry. Top each peach half generously with this meringue.

Baking Directions

Preheat oven to moderate, 325° F. Place pot roast and squash on lower shelf. At the end of 1½ hours, place potatoes and peaches on oven shelf directly above roast. At the end of an additional 1 hour of baking time, remove squash and prepare as directed. Leave meat, potatoes and peaches in oven to bake 30 minutes longer. Total oven time 3 hours.

POT ROAST GRAVY

¼ cup flour
¼ teaspoon salt
⅛ teaspoon pepper

¼ cup water
1 beef bouillon cube

Remove meat from roasting pan. Place pan over low heat on top-stove burner. Blend flour, salt, pepper and water; stir until smooth. Add this mixture and bouillon cube to hot broth in pan. Cook, stirring constantly, until smooth and thickened. Strain before serving.

Menu 31. Beef Loaf for Six
(60-MINUTE OVEN TIME)

RAW RELISH TRAY
BEEF LOAF   TOMATO GRAVY
BAKED NOODLES   BRUSSELS SPROUTS
CITRUS CAKE PUDDING   COFFEE

Beef Loaf

2 pounds ground round steak
1 pound ground lean pork steak
1½ cups soft bread crumbs
2 eggs
½ cup milk
1 teaspoon salt

⅛ teaspoon pepper
1 teaspoon monosodium glutamate
4 slices bacon
2 tablespoons flour
1 cup tomato cocktail

Have beef and pork ground together. Add bread crumbs. Knead lightly. Beat eggs slightly; add milk, salt, pepper and monosodium glutamate. Mix thoroughly with meat. Form in loaf and place in loaf pan. Lay bacon strips over meat. Remove bacon during last half hour of baking. When loaf is baked, remove from pan and drain off all but 2 tablespoons fat. On top of range add flour to last of fat, allowing flour to brown slightly. Add tomato cocktail and cook until thickened.

Baked Noodles

8 ounces (1 package) egg noodles
2 tablespoons butter
½ cup chopped green pepper
½ cup chopped onion

1 pimento, chopped
¼ teaspoon salt
⅛ teaspoon pepper
1 cup milk
2 eggs, beaten

Cook noodles; rinse in cold water and drain. Melt butter and add green pepper and onion, and cook until tender. Add to drained noodles the cooked onions and peppers, then the pimento, salt, pepper, milk and beaten eggs. Pour into round, greased, 9-inch baking pan.

Brussels Sprouts

2 packages frozen Brussels sprouts
½ cup water

2 tablespoons lemon juice
2 tablespoons butter
¼ teaspoon salt

Place frozen Brussels sprouts, water, lemon juice, butter and salt into saucepan. Cover tightly.

Citrus Cake Pudding

¼ cup butter
1 cup sugar
3 eggs, separated
¼ cup lemon juice
1 teaspoon grated lemon rind

⅓ cup flour
1 cup milk
⅛ teaspoon salt
2 oranges

Cream butter; add sugar, and cream together. Add beaten egg yolks, lemon juice and rind. Add flour and milk. Beat egg whites with salt until stiff but not dry. Fold into batter. Peel oranges, remove membrane and slice across in thirds. Grease 6 individual baking cups. Place orange slice in each cup and pour in batter. Set cups in pan of hot water.

Baking Directions

Preheat oven to moderate, 350° F. Place noodles and Brussels sprouts on lower shelf; on shelf directly above, place meat loaf and pudding. Total oven time 60 minutes.

Good Extra: Raw Relish Tray

2 carrots
1 stalk celery
2 tomatoes

Water cress
Pickles
Olives

Scrape carrots and cut into thin sticks. Wash celery, separating into individual stalks. Slice the tomatoes. Arrange attractively and garnish with water cress, pickles and olives on large serving tray or platter.

Menu 32. Deviled Steak for Six
(60-MINUTE OVEN TIME)

DEVILED STEAK

PAPRIKA POTATOES   SHREDDED BEETS

COLESLAW WITH SOUR CREAM (MENU 8)

CLOVERLEAF ROLLS *   BUTTER

PEACH RICE PUDDING   COFFEE

*(Buy these.)

Deviled Steak

1½ pounds ground beef	1½ teaspoons salt
1 cup milk	¼ teaspoon pepper
3 tablespoons finely-chopped onion	¼ teaspoon mustard
	1 tablespoon horse-radish
¾ cup cracker crumbs	6 strips bacon
2 tablespoons chopped parsley	6 thin slices sharp cheese

Mix together beef, milk, onion, crumbs and parsley. Blend salt, pepper and mustard, and add with horse-radish to beef. Mix thoroughly. Shape lightly into oblong patties. Wrap a strip of bacon around each and secure with picks. Place in shallow baking pan. During the last 15 minutes of baking place slice of cheese on each patty.

Paprika Potatoes

6 large potatoes	½ teaspoon paprika
¾ teaspoon salt	¼ cup melted butter
¼ teaspoon pepper	

Wash, pare and slice potatoes ⅛-inch thick. Into greased 2-quart casserole place layer of potatoes. Sprinkle with salt, pepper and paprika. Repeat until all potatoes are used. Over top of potatoes slowly pour melted butter. Cover tightly.

Shredded Beets

8 large beets	¼ cup melted butter
½ teaspoon salt	¼ cup water
¼ teaspoon pepper	1 teaspoon vinegar

Wash, peel and cut beets in strips. Place in greased, 1½-quart casserole. Season with salt and pepper. Combine butter, water and vinegar, and pour over beets. Cover tightly.

Peach Rice Pudding

2 cups cooked rice	1 tablespoon lemon juice
½ cup milk	6 peach halves
½ cup peach juice	¼ cup chopped nuts
1 egg	¼ cup confectioners sugar
¼ cup sugar	¼ cup chopped dates
1 tablespoon melted butter	1 tablespoon melted butter
¼ teaspoon grated lemon rind	

Mix together rice, milk and peach juice. Beat egg and add sugar, beating until blended. Combine rice and egg mixtures; add 1 tablespoon butter, lemon rind and juice. Pour into greased, 1½-quart baking dish. Arrange peach halves, hollow-side up, on top of rice. Mix together nuts, confectioners sugar, dates and second tablespoon of butter. Fill peach hollows with nut mixture.

Baking Directions

Preheat oven to moderate, 375° F. Place patties and potatoes on lower shelf. On shelf directly above, set beets and pudding. At the end of 45 minutes baking time remove pudding. Place rolls to heat, arrange cheese slices on patties and bake 15 minutes longer. Total oven time 60 minutes.

Menu 33. Dad's Favorite Dinner for Six

(55-MINUTE OVEN TIME)

RAW RELISH TRAY (MENU 31)
HAMBURGER PATTIES
MASHED POTATOES   SMOTHERED ONIONS
SALT STICKS *   BUTTER
MERINGUE BAKED APPLES   COFFEE

*(Buy these.)

Hamburger Patties

½ cup milk
3 tablespoons grated onion
1½ teaspoons salt
½ teaspoon sage

1½ cups soft bread crumbs
2 pounds hamburger
3 tablespoons flour
6 slices bacon

Add milk, grated onion, salt and sage to bread crumbs. Mix thoroughly. Add hamburger and blend thoroughly. Divide into 6 portions and shape into ¾-inch-thick patties. Flour lightly and wrap 1 slice bacon around each patty; fasten with toothpick. Place in greased 9-inch baking pan.

Mashed Potatoes

8 medium-sized potatoes
1 cup water
½ teaspoon salt

2 tablespoons butter
2 tablespoons hot milk
¼ teaspoon pepper

Pare potatoes and cut in quarters. Place in saucepan with water and salt. Cover tightly and bake. Before serving, mash free of lumps. Add butter, milk and pepper, and beat until fluffy.

Smothered Onions

12 large onions
¼ cup butter
¼ teaspoon salt
⅛ teaspoon pepper
2 tablespoons water

Peel and slice onions. Place in saucepan with butter, salt, pepper and water. Cover tightly.

Meringue Baked Apples

6 medium-sized baking apples
3 teaspoons butter
¾ cup brown sugar
¾ cup raisins
1½ cups orange juice
2 egg whites
2 tablespoons cold water
¼ cup sugar
½ teaspoon vanilla
⅛ teaspoon salt

Wash apples. Remove core and pare skin half way down sides. In center of each apple place ½ teaspoon butter, 2 tablespoons brown sugar and 2 tablespoons raisins. Place in greased, 9-inch baking pan. Pour orange juice around apples and bake. Then top each apple with meringue made by beating egg whites and water until stiff, adding sugar slowly, and then salt and vanilla.

Baking Directions

Preheat oven to moderate, 375° F. Place apples and potatoes on lower shelf; on shelf directly above, place hamburgers and onions. At the end of 40 minutes baking time, remove apples and top with meringue. Return to oven and bake 15 minutes longer. Total oven time 55 minutes.

78

Menu 34. Dutch Dinner Casserole for Six

(2-HOUR OVEN TIME)

DUTCH DINNER CASSEROLE   CONDIMENT TRAY
LETTUCE HEARTS AND CHILI SAUCE DRESSING (MENU 50)
NAPFKUCHEN (RICH COFFEECAKE)   ROYAL ANNE CHERRIES
EGG COFFEE

Dutch Casserole

2 pounds round steak
3 tablespoons shortening
3 tablespoons flour
1 teaspoon salt
¼ teaspoon pepper
1 cup drained tomato juice
    and water

6 medium-sized potatoes
12 small carrots
6 small onions
2½ cups (No. 2 can) tomatoes,
    drained

Cut steak into 1-inch cubes. Brown in hot shortening. Remove meat to 3-quart greased casserole. Add flour, salt and pepper to fat in pan, and stir until smooth. Slowly add juice and water. Cook 2 minutes. Place potatoes, carrots, onions and tomatoes on top of meat. Pour gravy over vegetables; cover tightly.

Napfkuchen (Rich Coffeecake)

1 package yeast
1¼ cups cold water
5 cups sifted flour
⅛ teaspoon salt
1 cup butter
1 cup sugar

6 eggs, separated
¾ cup scalded milk
1 cup raisins
½ cup currants
1 cup pecans

Add yeast to cold water and let stand 3 minutes. Sift flour and salt together. Cream butter, add sugar gradually and cream thoroughly. Add beaten yolks and beat until fluffy. Add 1 cup flour and mix thoroughly. Add yeast and blend. Alternately, add remaining flour and milk. Beat well. Fold in stiffly beaten egg whites, raisins, currants and pecans. Pour into well-greased 12-inch angel-cake pan. Allow to double in bulk before baking.

KUCHEN GLAZE

4 tablespoons confectioners
   sugar
1 tablespoon butter, melted

1 tablespoon milk
¼ teaspoon vanilla

Blend together and frost coffeecake while it is still warm.

Baking Directions

Preheat oven to moderate, 350° F. Place meat on lower shelf; on shelf directly above, place raised kuchen. At the end of 1 hour baking time, remove kuchen. Continue baking meat 1 hour longer. Total oven time 2 hours.

Egg Coffee

6 cups water
7 tablespoons regular-grind
   coffee

Few grains salt
1 whole egg
¼ cup cold water

Boil water. Blend coffee, salt and egg, including crushed shell. Stir into boiling water. Boil 7 minutes. Slowly add cold water to settle grounds.

Menu 35. Glorified Hamburg Roll for Four

(50-MINUTE OVEN TIME)

HAMBURG ROLL WITH TOMATO SAUCE

WHIPPED POTATOES   PURPLE CABBAGE WITH APPLE

RYE BREAD *   BUTTER

BANANA PUDDING   CHOCOLATE WAFERS *   COFFEE

*(Buy these.)

Hamburg Roll with Tomato Sauce

1½ pounds ground round steak

2 cups bread crumbs

1 tablespoon onion juice

½ teaspoon salt

⅛ teaspoon pepper

1 egg, beaten

6 large stuffed olives, sliced

2 hard-cooked eggs

1 cup tomatoes

½ cup sliced onions

1 tablespoon butter

1 cup hot water

Mix meat with crumbs, onion juice, salt, pepper and beaten egg. Pat mixture into rectangular shape on work board. Arrange olives and sliced hard-cooked eggs across one end of meat. Roll meat around them tightly. Place in loaf pan. Mix tomatoes, onions, butter and hot water. Pour over roll. To serve, slice crosswise.

Whipped Potatoes

4 large potatoes

½ cup water

½ teaspoon salt

¼ teaspoon pepper

2 tablespoons butter

2 tablespoons hot milk

Wash, pare and cut potatoes in fourths. Place in saucepan with water. Cover tightly. Before serving, drain, mash and season with salt, pepper, butter and milk. Whip with fork until fluffy.

Purple Cabbage with Apple

1 small head purple cabbage	2 bouillon cubes
3 slices bacon	½ teaspoon salt
1 medium-sized onion, sliced	⅛ teaspoon pepper
2 tart apples	2 teaspoons brown sugar
1½ cups boiling water	1 teaspoon vinegar

Wash and shred cabbage. Fry bacon until crisp. Remove bacon and fry onion until tender and slightly browned. Chop bacon. Add to cabbage the chopped bacon, browned onion, bacon fat, peeled and thickly-sliced apples. Toss until well mixed. Place in greased 2-quart casserole. Dissolve bouillon cubes in boiling water; add salt, pepper, brown sugar and vinegar. Pour over cabbage. Cover tightly.

Banana Pudding

4 bananas	1 egg
2 tablespoons butter	1 egg yolk
¼ cup sugar	½ cup top milk
1 teaspoon lemon juice	Confectioners sugar
¼ teaspoon grated lemon rind	

Mash bananas. Cream butter; gradually add sugar, lemon juice and rind. Fold in banana pulp. Beat egg and egg yolk slightly. Add milk and add to banana mixture. Turn into 1-quart buttered mold. Place in pan with water 1½ inches deep. Serve, well dusted with confectioners sugar.

Baking Directions

Preheat oven to moderate, 350° F. Place potatoes and cabbage on lower shelf; on shelf directly above, place pudding and beef roll. Bake everything 50 minutes.

Menu 36. Meat Loaf Dinner for Six

(60-MINUTE OVEN TIME)

MEAT LOAF   DILL PICKLES

BAKED SWEET POTATOES   CAULIFLOWER SUPREME

HOT CRUSTY ROLLS *   BUTTER

BAKED PEARS   LADYFINGERS *   COFFEE

*(Buy these.)

Meat Loaf

2 pounds ground beef, pork and veal
½ cup fine bread crumbs
½ cup milk
2 teaspoons salt
¼ teaspoon pepper
1 egg, slightly beaten
2 tablespoons finely-chopped onion

⅛ teaspoon celery salt
⅛ teaspoon garlic salt
½ cup chili sauce
1 teaspoon prepared horse-radish
1 small onion, cut into rings
4 slices bacon, cut in half

Combine meat, bread crumbs, milk, salt, pepper, egg, onion, celery salt, garlic salt, chili sauce and horse-radish. Toss together lightly and shape into round loaf about 8 inches across and 3 inches thick. Place in greased 9-inch cake pan; top with onion rings and bacon strips.

Cauliflower Supreme

1 medium-sized head cauli-flower
1 quart boiling water
1 teaspoon salt
2 tablespoons milk
1 cup stale bread crumbs

½ cup butter
1 teaspoon finely-chopped onion
¼ teaspoon salt
⅛ teaspoon pepper

Place cauliflower, head down, in cold water; soak 15 minutes. Remove leaves and stalk from head and place in boiling water with 1 teaspoon salt and 2 tablespoons milk. Cook until just tender, about 20 minutes. Drain and place in greased, shallow baking pan. Brown bread crumbs in the butter and add the chopped onion, ¼ teaspoon salt and pepper. Pour this crumb sauce over cauliflower.

Baked Sweet Potatoes

6 large sweet potatoes   1 tablespoon shortening

Wash sweet potatoes well and grease with shortening. Prick each with a fork to prevent bursting in oven.

Baked Pears

6 canned pear halves, drained   2 tablespoons tart jam
¼ cup peanut butter   1 cup fine stale cake crumbs
¼ cup pear juice   3 marshmallows, cut in half

Place pear halves, cut-side up, in greased 8-inch baking pan. Blend peanut butter, pear juice, jam and cake crumbs. Fill each pear half with this mixture and top each with marshmallow half. Serve with cold pear juice.

Baking Directions

Preheat oven to moderate, 375° F. Place meat loaf and sweet potatoes on lower shelf. At the end of 30 minutes, set cauliflower and pears on shelf directly above meat loaf and potatoes; continue baking 30 minutes longer. Add rolls to heat for last ten minutes. Total oven time 60 minutes.

Menu 37. Spanish Beef for Four
(53-MINUTE OVEN TIME)

SPANISH BEEF   BAKED SUMMER SQUASH
WHOLE-WHEAT BREAD *   BUTTER
FROZEN VEGETABLE SALAD (MENU 24)
PINEAPPLE JELLY ROLL   COFFEE

*(Buy this.)

Spanish Beef

1 pound ground beef
1 green pepper, chopped
1 onion, chopped
2 tablespoons butter
2 cups cooked broad noodles
1 cup tomato soup
1 cup water
½ teaspoon salt

½ cup button mushrooms, sliced
1 teaspoon Worcestershire sauce
½ teaspoon paprika
¼ teaspoon pepper
¾ cup grated Italian cheese

Brown beef, green pepper and onion in butter. Place 1 cup of noodles in greased 2-quart casserole. Top with half the beef mixture, add remaining noodles for third layer and top with rest of beef. Combine other ingredients, blend thoroughly and pour over layers in casserole.

Baked Summer Squash

1 small onion, diced
2 tablespoons butter
1 hard-cooked egg, chopped
2 summer squash, diced

1 egg, beaten
2 tablespoons light cream
2 tablespoons fine bread crumbs

Cook onion in butter until tender; combine with chopped egg, squash and beaten egg. Blend well and pour into 8 by 11 inch baking pan; pour over cream and sprinkle with bread crumbs.

Pineapple Jelly Roll

5 eggs separated	1 cup sifted cake flour
1 cup sugar	¼ teaspoon salt
1 tablespoon lemon rind	Confectioners sugar
2 tablespoons lemon juice	

Beat egg whites until stiff but not dry; add ½ cup of the sugar, slowly beating until stiff enough to hold in peaks. Beat egg yolks until thick, add remaining ½ cup sugar, lemon rind and juice; blend thoroughly. Fold egg-yolk mixture into beaten egg whites. Sift flour and salt together and fold egg mixture into dry ingredients. Line jelly-roll pan with waxed paper or aluminum foil and grease well. Pour batter into pan. When baked, loosen sides of cake from pan and turn out on cloth sprinkled with confectioners sugar. Roll as tightly as possible and wrap in towel. Set aside to cool. When cooled, unroll, spread with pineapple filling and roll up again.

PINEAPPLE FILLING

¼ cup sugar	3½ cups (No. 2½ can)
2 tablespoons cornstarch	crushed pineapple

Blend sugar and cornstarch; stir into pineapple. Cook until thickened, stirring constantly. Chill before spreading on cake.

Baking Directions

Preheat oven to 375° F. Place Spanish beef on lower shelf in oven and jelly roll on shelf directly above. At the end of 18 minutes baking time, remove jelly roll and add squash. Continue baking 35 minutes longer. Total oven time 53 minutes.

Menu 38. Swiss Steak for Four

(2-HOUR OVEN TIME)

SPECIAL SWISS STEAK   PICKLE RELISH

BAKED POTATOES   GREEN BEANS WITH BACON

ZUCCHINI   PARKER HOUSE ROLLS *   BUTTER

CHOCOLATE ICE CREAM   SPONGE CAKES *   COFFEE

* (Buy these.)

Special Swiss Steak

¼ cup flour	4 tablespoons fat or salad oil
1 teaspoon salt	1 tablespoon onion juice
¼ teaspoon pepper	1 cup dry vermouth
1½ pounds round steak, 1 inch thick	½ cup water
	12 large green olives

Combine flour, salt and pepper. Spread half of this mixture on board and lay steak on top of it. Sprinkle the remaining flour on steak. Pound flour into steak, using a potato masher or edge of plate. Brown in fat or salad oil. Remove and place in casserole. Add onion juice, ½ cup of vermouth and water. 15 minutes before steak is done, add remaining vermouth and olives. During baking, add hot water if needed to prevent sticking. Thicken sauce for gravy.

Baked Potatoes

4 baking potatoes   1 tablespoon shortening

Wash potatoes with stiff brush. Prick with fork to prevent bursting. Rub with shortening. Place in shallow baking pan.

Green Beans with Bacon

4 slices bacon, lean	2 stalks celery, French-cut
1 package French-style frozen	1/8 teaspoon salt
beans	1/8 teaspoon pepper

Fry bacon; place with drippings in casserole. Place unthawed beans over bacon; add celery, salt and pepper. Cover tightly.

Zucchini

4 small zucchini	1/8 teaspoon basil
1 clove garlic	1/4 cup water
1/4 cup olive oil	1 tablespoon lemon juice

Wash and scrape and slice zucchini. Brown garlic in olive oil in saucepan. Remove garlic; add basil. Add zucchini and water. Cover tightly. Pour lemon juice over zucchini at serving time.

Baking Directions

Preheat oven to moderate, 350° F. Place steak on lower shelf. At the end of 1 hour, set potatoes on same shelf. On shelf directly above, place zucchini and beans. Bake 1 hour longer. Total oven time 2 hours. Heat rolls while making gravy.

Essential Extra: Good Gravy

Remove Swiss steak from casserole. Measure remaining liquid. For each cup of liquid, blend together 2½ tablespoons flour and 1/4 cup water. Add to stock. Cook until smooth and thickened, about 10 minutes.

88

Menu 39. Corned Beef Casserole for Four

(90-MINUTE OVEN TIME)

ORANGE-NUT BREAD   CREAM-CHEESE SPREAD
CRISP SALAD GREENS WITH CUCUMBER
SOUR CREAM DRESSING (MENU 61)
APPLE TAPIOCA PUDDING

Corned Beef Casserole

1 can corned beef
4 potatoes
4 carrots
2 onions

1 large green pepper
¼ teaspoon salt
1 can condensed tomato soup
⅓ can water

Cut corned beef into 4 slices. Cut each slice in half. Place in greased 2-quart casserole. Pare and slice potatoes and carrots and peel onions. Remove seeds from pepper and slice. Arrange vegetables in layers over corned beef. Season with salt. Dilute soup with water and pour over vegetables. Cover.

Orange-Nut Bread

2 teaspoons grated orange rind
½ cup orange juice
½ cup boiling water
1 cup chopped dates
1 cup sugar
2 tablespoons butter
1 teaspoon vanilla

2 cups sifted all-purpose flour
1 teaspoon baking powder
1 teaspoon baking soda
¼ teaspoon salt
1 egg, beaten
½ cup walnuts, chopped fine

Mix together orange rind, juice, water, dates, sugar, butter and vanilla. Let stand 3 minutes. Sift together flour, baking powder, soda and salt. Add beaten egg to orange mixture; add sifted dry ingredients. Beat thoroughly. Stir in nut meats. Pour into greased loaf pan.

Apple Tapioca Pudding

1 cup water	2 tablespoons butter
½ cup pearl tapioca	2 eggs separated
4 medium-sized apples	¼ cup sugar
¼ cup brown sugar	¼ teaspoon salt
¼ cup raisins	¼ teaspoon nutmeg
2 cups milk	2 tablespoons lemon juice

Add water to tapioca and allow to stand for 1 hour. Pare and core apples. Fill cavities with brown sugar and raisins; place in 1½-quart greased casserole. To the soaked tapioca add milk and butter and cook over hot water until clear. Pour over beaten egg yolks. Add sugar, salt and nutmeg, and mix well. Add lemon juice. Fold in beaten egg whites. Pour over apples and bake.

Baking Directions

Preheat oven to moderate, 350° F. Place corned beef casserole on lower shelf; on shelf directly above, place orange bread and tapioca pudding. At the end of 1 hour baking time, remove bread and pudding. Bake corned beef 30 minutes longer. Total oven time 90 minutes.

Menu 40. Barbecued Frankfurters for Four

(20-MINUTE OVEN TIME)

BARBECUED FRANKFURTERS

SLICED DILL PICKLES   CELERY

POTATO CAKES   FRENCH FRIED ONION RINGS

HOT FRENCH BREAD *   BUTTER

PEACH MERINGUES   COFFEE

* (Buy this.)

Barbecued Frankfurters

6 frankfurters
2 tablespoons bacon fat
1/3 cup chopped onion
1/2 teaspoon paprika
1/4 teaspoon pepper
1 teaspoon dry mustard

1/16 teaspoon cayenne pepper
2 tablespoons sugar
2 tablespoons vinegar
3 tablespoons catsup
3 tablespoons Worcestershire
sauce

Split frankfurters lengthwise. Place in 9- by 12-inch greased baking pan. Melt fat, add onion and simmer until tender. Add remaining ingredients and simmer 2 minutes. Pour sauce over frankfurters.

Potato Cakes

2 cups mashed potatoes
1 egg yolk
1/4 teaspoon salt

1/8 teaspoon pepper
1 1/2 tablespoons cream
4 tablespoons butter

Mix all ingredients together. Shape into 4 flat cakes. Place in shallow 8-inch, greased pan. Top with butter.

French Fried Onion Rings

1 package frozen French fried   ⅛ teaspoon salt
    onion rings

Spread out onion rings in shallow baking pan. Before serving, salt lightly.

Peach Meringues

4 large canned peach halves
4 large graham crackers,
    crushed
¼ teaspoon cinnamon
¼ teaspoon ground cloves
2 tablespoons butter, melted

2 tablespoons peanut butter
1 tablespoon lemon juice
2 egg whites
2 tablespoons cold water
¼ cup sugar
¼ teaspoon almond extract

Place peach halves in greased 8-inch pie plate. To the crushed crackers add cinnamon and cloves. Blend. Mix butter, peanut butter and lemon juice together. Add to crackers and mix well. Pack mixture into peach cavities. Top with meringue made by beating egg whites and water until stiff. Then slowly add sugar and continue beating to stiff meringue. Add almond extract. Pile on filled peaches. Serve warm.

Baking Directions

Preheat oven to hot, 400° F. Place frankfurters and onion rings on lower shelf. On shelf directly above, place peaches and potato cakes. Bake everything 20 minutes. Warm bread in oven after heat has been turned off.

Menu 41. Frankfurter Budget Dinner for Four

(75-MINUTE OVEN TIME)

FRANKFURTER CROWN ROAST   RAW RELISH TRAY (MENU 31)
POTATO-AND-ONION CASSEROLE   RED CABBAGE IN WINE
CRACKED-WHEAT BREAD *   BUTTER
BUTTER PECAN ICE CREAM   PREPARED-MIX WHITE CAKE (MENU 51)
COFFEE

*(Buy this.)

Frankfurter Crown Roast

12 frankfurters
2 eighteen-inch pieces of string
½ cup French dressing
4 cups stale bread crumbs
¾ teaspoon salt
¼ teaspoon pepper

½ teaspoon poultry seasoning
1 tablespoon chopped parsley
½ cup orange juice
1 egg, beaten
¼ pound sausage meat
½ cup celery, cut fine

String frankfurters together on 2 eighteen-inch pieces of string so that curved sides are in one direction. Use one string 2 inches from the top of each frankfurter, the other 2 inches from bottom of each frankfurter. Lay flat in baking pan. Cover with French dressing; turn once while preparing dressing. Toss together bread crumbs, salt, pepper, poultry seasoning and parsley. Combine orange juice and egg. Add to bread mixture and blend. Fry sausage meat until browned and crumbly. Drain off all but 2 tablespoons of sausage fat. Add with celery to dressing. Remove frankfurters from French dressing; tie ends of string to form a crown. Pack dressing in hollow of crown. Place, standing, in 8-inch baking pan.

Potato-and-Onion Casserole

5 medium-sized potatoes
1 Spanish onion
¼ teaspoon salt

1 can condensed tomato soup
½ can water

Pare and thinly slice potatoes and onion. Place alternate layers of potatoes and onions in greased 2-quart casserole. Sprinkle with salt. Mix soup with ½ can water; pour over vegetables and bake.

Red Cabbage in Wine

4 cups shredded red cabbage
1 cup diced tart apples
2 tablespoons bacon fat, melted
2 tablespoons vinegar

½ cup water
½ cup red wine
2 tablespoons brown sugar
½ teaspoon salt
¼ teaspoon pepper

Place layers of cabbage and apples in Dutch oven. Add bacon fat, vinegar, water and wine. Sprinkle with brown sugar, salt and pepper. Cover tightly.

Baking Directions

Preheat oven to moderate, 350° F. Place potato-and-onion casserole on lower shelf in oven. Place pan of white cake on shelf above. At the end of 30 minutes, remove cake and place crown roast on same shelf. Set red cabbage on lower shelf. Bake 45 minutes longer. Total oven time 75 minutes.

Menu 42. Liver Pot Roast for Six

(90-MINUTE OVEN TIME)

LIVER POT ROAST

WHIPPED POTATOES   SOUTHERN CORN

HOT CRESCENT ROLLS *   BUTTER

TOSSED SALAD WITH ROQUEFORT DRESSING (MENU 54)

CHOCOLATE PUDDING WITH VANILLA ICE CREAM   COFFEE

* (Buy these.)

Liver Pot Roast

1½-pounds beef liver *in one piece*

2 tablespoons flour

½ teaspoon salt

¼ teaspoon pepper

¼ teaspoon dry mustard

½ cup fat

3 large onions, sliced

½ teaspoon salt

½ teaspoon paprika

⅛ teaspoon celery salt

¾ cup sour cream

½ cup water

Wipe liver with damp cloth. Rub with flour mixed with salt, pepper and mustard. Brown in hot fat. Place browned liver in greased casserole. Brown onions in remaining fat, and arrange over liver. Combine remaining ingredients with fat left in pan and blend well. Pour over liver and onions. Cover casserole tightly.

Whipped Potatoes

6 medium-sized potatoes

1 cup water

½ teaspoon salt

2 tablespoons butter

3 tablespoons hot milk

⅛ teaspoon pepper

Pare potatoes and cut in half. Place in saucepan with water and salt. Cover tightly. Before serving, drain, mash and season with butter, milk and pepper. Whip with fork.

Southern Corn

1½ cups canned whole-kernel corn
1½ cups cracker crumbs
2 cups milk
3 eggs, separated

1 green pepper
2 tablespoons butter
½ teaspoon salt
⅛ teaspoon pepper
6 slices bacon

Mix together corn, cracker crumbs, milk, and beaten egg yolks. Seed and dice green pepper and simmer in butter until tender. Add to corn. Add salt and pepper. Fold in beaten egg whites. Pour into 8-inch, greased baking pan. Top with bacon strips.

Chocolate Pudding

3 cups milk
1 tablespoon butter
¾ cup sugar
1 tablespoon cocoa

4½ cups corn flakes
2 eggs, beaten
1 teaspoon vanilla

Scald milk and butter. Mix together the sugar and cocoa. Add hot milk and corn flakes. Add to beaten eggs and vanilla. Pour into greased 1½-quart casserole. Serve with vanilla ice cream.

Baking Directions

Preheat oven to moderate, 325° F. Place roast on lower shelf; on shelf directly above, place chocolate pudding. After 30 minutes, set potatoes on shelf with liver and place corn on shelf with pudding. Bake 1 hour longer. Total oven time 90 minutes. Heat the rolls while you make the gravy.

Menu 43. Baked Liverburger Luncheon for Six

(60-MINUTE OVEN TIME)

BAKED LIVERBURGERS

CURRIED RICE AND ONIONS

HOT FRENCH BREAD * BUTTER

APPLESAUCE SALAD

RUM SQUARES WITH VANILLA ICE CREAM TEA

*(Buy this.)

Baked Liverburgers

1½ pounds liver

3 cups boiling water

⅓ cup fine cracker crumbs

¼ cup bacon fat

¼ cup tomato purée

1 egg, well beaten

1 teaspoon salt

¼ teaspoon pepper

¼ cup finely-chopped onion

6 bacon strips

Cover liver with boiling water; let stand 2 minutes. Drain and dry liver; put through food chopper. Add remaining ingredients, except bacon, in order given; blend well and shape into 6 patties about 2 inches thick. Wrap a strip of bacon around each patty and secure with toothpick. Place in greased 9-inch baking pan.

Curried Rice and Onions

2 Spanish onions, sliced thick

2 cups boiling water

3 cups cooked rice

½ cup evaporated milk

½ teaspoon curry powder

⅛ teaspoon nutmeg

¼ teaspoon salt

3 tablespoons melted butter

Cook sliced onions in boiling water for 5 minutes. Drain onions well, combine with remaining ingredients and place in greased 1-quart casserole.

Rum Squares

½ cup shortening
1 cup light brown sugar
2 eggs, well beaten
2 teaspoons rum flavoring
1 cup cake flour

1 teaspoon baking powder
½ teaspoon salt
¼ cup milk
1 cup chopped walnuts

Cream shortening and sugar, add well-beaten eggs and rum flavoring, and blend well. Sift flour, baking powder and salt together and add alternately with milk to creamed mixture. Fold in chopped walnuts and pour into greased, waxed-paper-lined, 8-inch-square baking pan.

Baking Directions

Preheat oven to slow, 300° F. Place liverburgers and rum squares on lower shelf, leaving room on the same shelf for curried rice. At the end of 30 minutes, place the curried rice on lowest shelf and French bread on shelf directly above. Continue baking 30 minutes longer. Total baking time 60 minutes.

Delicious Extra: Applesauce Salad

1 cup applesauce
⅔ cup pineapple chunks, drained
½ cup water

1 package lime-flavored gelatine
½ head lettuce
1 cup cottage cheese

Combine applesauce, pineapple chunks and water; bring to a boil and boil 1 minute. Remove from heat and stir in lime gelatine. Rinse 6 individual molds in cold water and fill with gelatine mixture; place in refrigerator until firm. Unmold each on bed of lettuce and top with cottage cheese and salad dressing.

Menu 44. Braised Beef Tongue for Six
(90-MINUTE OVEN TIME)

BRAISED BEEF TONGUE WITH RAISINS   MIXED SWEET PICKLES
BAKED POTATOES   CARROTS AND PEAS
MELBA TOAST *   BUTTER
CHOCOLATE SOUFFLÉ WITH MINT-FLAVORED WHIPPED CREAM
VANILLA WAFERS *   COFFEE

*(Buy these.)

Braised Beef Tongue

4-pound tongue	2 carrots, sliced
2 quarts cold water	1 bay leaf
1 teaspoon salt	⅛ teaspoon thyme
2 quarts boiling water	1½ cups raisins
1 stalk celery	½ cup red wine
2 medium-sized onions, sliced	

Cover tongue with cold water; add salt and simmer 1½ hours. Drain. Cover with fresh boiling water. Add celery, onions, carrots, bay leaf and thyme. Simmer 1½ hours. Remove tongue. Skin and trim off roots. Cut in ⅓-inch slices. Place in casserole. Place raisins in wire strainer; steam over hot water 5 minutes to plump. Arrange plumped raisins over sliced tongue. Pour red wine over raisins.

Baked Potatoes

6 Idaho potatoes	3 tablespoons butter
1 tablespoon shortening	¼ teaspoon paprika

Scrub potatoes with stiff brush; dry. Rub with shortening and prick with sharp fork. Place in baking pan. Bake.

Carrots and Peas

2 packages frozen carrots and peas	½ cup water
	¼ teaspoon sugar
2 tablespoons butter	2 tablespoons cream

Place butter, water, sugar and carrots and peas in saucepan; cover tightly.

Note: Before serving, toss with cream.

Chocolate Soufflé

2 tablespoons butter	2 one-ounce squares chocolate,
3 tablespoons flour	melted
¼ teaspoon salt	3 eggs, separated
1 cup milk, scalded	⅓ cup sugar
	1 teaspoon vanilla

Melt butter; add flour and salt. Stir until smooth. Add hot milk slowly. Add melted chocolate. Cook, stirring constantly, until smooth. Beat egg yolks and sugar; slowly add hot chocolate mixture. Blend thoroughly; cool. Beat egg whites and vanilla until stiff but not dry. Fold into cooled chocolate mixture. Pour into well-greased pudding pan; set in a pan of hot water and bake. Serve at once.

MINT-FLAVORED WHIPPED CREAM

½ pint heavy cream	¼ teaspoon mint flavoring
3 tablespoons sugar	

Beat cream until slightly stiff, add mint. Add sugar slowly and beat until stiff.

Baking Directions

Preheat oven to hot, 425° F. Place potatoes on lower shelf. After 30 minutes, place carrots and peas on shelf with potatoes. Place tongue on shelf directly above. Reduce heat to moderate, 325°. Bake 25 minutes longer. Remove potatoes, carrots and peas and tongue, and serve. Place soufflé on shelf in center of oven. Bake 35 minutes. Total oven time 90 minutes.

Menu 45. Baked Kidney Lamb Chops for Six

(45-MINUTE OVEN TIME)

BAKED KIDNEY LAMB CHOPS   MINT JELLY

FRENCH FRIED POTATOES   PARSLEY BUTTERED CARROTS

SALT STICKS *   BUTTER

APPLE CRUNCH   CREAM   COFFEE

(ALMOND COOKIES FOR TOMORROW)

*(Buy these.)

Baked Kidney Lamb Chops

6 two-inch kidney lamb chops
1½ cups boiling water
1 slice lemon
1½ cups soft bread crumbs
½ teaspoon sage
¼ teaspoon salt

⅛ teaspoon pepper
1 tablespoon chopped parsley
2 tablespoons milk
6 strips bacon
½ cup white wine or water

Remove kidneys from chops. Leave tail of chop attached. Pour boiling water over kidneys. Add slice of lemon; simmer 10 minutes. Drain and chop kidneys. Blend together bread crumbs, chopped kidneys, sage, salt, pepper, parsley and milk. Pack dressing into opening left in chops after removal of kidneys. Wrap bacon strip around each chop and dressing; secure with toothpick. Place chops in greased 9- by 12-inch baking pan and add wine.

French Fried Potatoes

2 boxes frozen French fried potatoes

¼ teaspoon salt

Spread out frozen French fried potatoes in baking pan. Before serving, sprinkle with salt.

Parsley Buttered Carrots

8 medium-sized carrots
2 tablespoons butter
¼ teaspoon salt
⅛ teaspoon pepper

2 tablespoons dried parsley
1/16 teaspoon nutmeg
½ cup water

Scrape and cut carrots into thin slices. Place butter, salt, pepper, parsley, nutmeg and water in saucepan. Add carrots; cover tightly.

Apple Crunch

1 cup brown sugar	2 tablespoons lemon juice
1 tablespoon flour	1½ cups quick-cooking
½ teaspoon nutmeg	oatmeal
¼ teaspoon cinnamon	⅓ cup sugar
¼ teaspoon mace	⅓ cup melted butter
6 cups thinly-sliced apples	

Blend together brown sugar, flour, nutmeg, cinnamon and mace. Pour over sliced apples and toss until apples are coated. Put into greased 9-inch baking pan. Sprinkle with lemon juice. Blend oatmeal, sugar and butter to form crumbs; pack on top of apples. Serve with cream.

Almond Cookies for Tomorrow

½ cup shortening	½ cup blanched almonds,
⅔ cup confectioners sugar	shredded
½ teaspoon vanilla	1¼ cups sifted cake flour
¼ teaspoon almond extract	⅛ teaspoon salt
1 egg yolk	

Cream shortening and sugar. Add vanilla and almond extract. Add egg yolk and beat. Fold in almonds, flour and salt. Roll about a third inch thick on floured board. Cut with 2-inch cooky cutter. Place on greased cooky sheet.

Baking Directions

Preheat oven to moderate, 350° F. Place chops and carrots on lower shelf. On shelf directly above, place apple crunch and cover with baking pan. At the end of 20 minutes remove cookies and place potatoes on top shelf and bake 25 minutes longer. Total baking time 45 minutes.

Note: Potatoes should be stirred once during baking time.

Menu 46. Roast Lamb for Six
(2½-HOUR OVEN TIME)

CHICKEN BROTH WITH RICE   SALTINES

ROAST LAMB   BROWN GRAVY

PAN ROAST POTATOES

HARVARD BEETS   MINTED PEAS

HARD ROLLS *   BUTTER

FIG PUDDING WITH VANILLA ICE CREAM   COFFEE

*(Buy these.)

Roast Lamb

5-pound leg of lamb

2 teaspoons salt

½ teaspoon pepper

¼ teaspoon dry mustard

2 tablespoons flour

Wipe lamb with damp cloth. Blend salt, pepper, mustard and flour; rub into leg of lamb. Place on rack in baking pan. If fell (or tough outer skin) is left on during roasting, remove before serving.

Harvard Beets

2 bunches fresh beets

¾ cup water

3 tablespoons butter

3 tablespoons flour

½ cup sugar

⅔ cup water from beets

⅓ cup vinegar

¼ teaspoon salt

Wash, pare and slice beets. Place in 2-quart casserole dish with ¾ cup water; cover tightly and bake. At the end of baking time, melt butter in saucepan, add flour and stir smooth. Add sugar, water from cooked beets, vinegar and salt. Cook together until smooth and clear, stirring constantly. Pour sauce over cooked beets.

Minted Peas

2 tablespoons butter	2 packages frozen peas
¼ cup water	¼ teaspoon salt
4 fresh mint leaves	⅛ teaspoon pepper

Place butter, water, mint leaves and frozen peas in 1½-quart casserole; cover tightly. When baked and ready to serve, season with salt and pepper.

Pan Roast Potatoes

12 small potatoes	2 tablespoons melted shortening

Peel and grease potatoes; place in pan around roast lamb.

Fig Pudding

2 cups dry coarse bread crumbs	1 teaspoon lemon juice
1 quart hot milk	¼ cup melted butter
¾ cup sugar	3 eggs, beaten
1 cup chopped figs	⅛ teaspoon salt
	½ cup coarsely chopped nuts

Combine crumbs and hot milk in large mixing bowl and set aside to cool to room temperature. When cooled, add remaining ingredients in order given; pour into greased 2-quart casserole.

Baking Directions

Preheat oven to moderate, 350° F. Place lamb on lower shelf. At the end of 1½ hours baking time, place potatoes around lamb and beets next to lamb. Place peas and fig pudding on shelf directly above, and continue baking 1 hour longer. Total baking time 2½ hours. Warm rolls in oven after heat has been turned off.

104

Menu 47. Ham and Sweet Surprise for Four
(25-MINUTE OVEN TIME)

HAM AND SWEET SURPRISE

SPINACH SPECIALTY   BAKED TOMATO HALVES

TIP-TOP MUFFINS   BUTTER

AVOCADO AND GRAPEFRUIT SALAD

RASPBERRY FLUFF   COFFEE

Ham and Sweet Surprise

1-pound can precooked ham
1½ cups mashed sweet
  potatoes

1 cup applesauce
3 tablespoons brown sugar
⅛ teaspoon ground cloves

Cut ham in ¼-inch-thick slices. Place in 9-inch greased baking pan and spread with mashed sweet potatoes. Top with applesauce and sprinkle with mixture of brown sugar and ground cloves.

Spinach Specialty

2 cups cooked spinach,
  chopped
3 tablespoons butter, melted
½ teaspoon salt

¼ teaspoon nutmeg
2 eggs, beaten
⅓ cup grated Italian-style
  cheese

Combine all ingredients, blend thoroughly and pour into 1-quart greased casserole.

Baked Tomato Halves

2 large tomatoes
½ teaspoon salt

¼ teaspoon pepper
2 teaspoons butter

Wash tomatoes well and cut in half crosswise. Place cut side up in greased 8-inch baking pan; sprinkle with salt and pepper and dot with butter.

Tip-Top Muffins

¼ cup shortening	4 teaspoons baking powder
⅓ cup sugar	1 teaspoon salt
1 egg, separated	1 cup milk
2 cups sifted all-purpose flour	

Cream shortening and sugar; add egg yolk and beat well. Sift flour, baking powder and salt together and add alternately with milk. Fold in stiffly-beaten egg white. Grease 8 large muffin cups and fill ⅔ full.

Baking Directions

Preheat oven to hot, 400° F. Place ham and spinach on lower shelf, and on shelf directly above place tomatoes and muffins. Bake everything 25 minutes.

Colorful Dessert: Raspberry Fluff

1 egg white	1 cup crushed raspberries
⅛ teaspoon salt	⅓ cup whole raspberries
¼ cup sugar	¼ cup grated cocoanut

Beat egg white until stiff, gradually adding salt and sugar. Fold in crushed raspberries and pile into 4 dessert dishes. Garnish with whole berries and coconut.

Tangy Addition: Avocado and Grapefruit Salad

1 grapefruit	4 lettuce cups
1 avocado	⅓ cup French dressing

Section grapefruit, saving all juice. Pare and slice avocado and dip in juice. Arrange slices alternately in lettuce cups. Serve with French dressing.

Menu 48. Ham Slice Supper for Four
(60-MINUTE OVEN TIME)

GRAPEFRUIT JUICE

HAM SLICE WITH PINEAPPLE

BAKED SWEET POTATOES   BAKED BRUSSELS SPROUTS

DARK RYE BREAD *   BUTTER

DATE-NUT LOAF WITH WHIPPED CREAM   COFFEE

*(Buy this.)

Ham Slice with Pineapple

2-pound ham slice, 1 inch thick	2 tablespoons brown sugar
8 whole cloves	1 tablespoon maraschino cherry juice
1 cup crushed pineapple, including juice	4 maraschino cherries

Place ham slice in greased 5- by 8-inch baking pan and press cloves into ham. Sprinkle with crushed pineapple, brown sugar, cherry juice and garnish with whole cherries.

Baked Sweet Potatoes

4 medium-sized sweet potatoes	1 teaspoon shortening

Wash and dry potatoes. Coat each well with shortening and prick with fork to prevent bursting in oven. Arrange potatoes in 9-inch baking pan.

Baked Brussels Sprouts

3 tablespoons butter, melted
2 tablespoons water
1 teaspoon meat extract

½ teaspoon salt
1 package frozen Brussels
    sprouts

Combine melted butter, water, meat extract and salt; place in 1-quart casserole with frozen Brussels sprouts and cover tightly.

Date-Nut Loaf

3 eggs
1 cup sugar
½ teaspoon vanilla
¼ cup all-purpose flour
¼ teaspoon salt

1 teaspoon baking powder
½ teaspoon nutmeg
1 cup chopped dates
1 cup chopped nuts
½ pint heavy cream, whipped

Beat eggs, gradually add sugar and vanilla. Sift dry ingredients together and stir into egg mixture. Fold in chopped dates and nuts. Blend well and pour batter into 4 large, greased custard cups. Place cups in baking pan and pour warm water around them to a depth of 1 inch. When serving, unmold and top with whipped cream.

Baking Directions

Preheat oven to moderate, 350° F. Place sweet potatoes on lower shelf and place ham slice and date-nut loaf on shelf directly above. At the end of 30 minutes, set Brussels sprouts on shelf with sweet potatoes. Continue baking 30 minutes longer. Total baking time 60 minutes.

Menu 49. Ham and Potato in Mustard Sauce for Four
(60-MINUTE OVEN TIME)

BAKED HAM IN MUSTARD SAUCE
BUTTERED FRENCH-STYLE GREEN BEANS   HEATED HARD ROLLS
BUTTER
APPLESAUCE SALAD (MENU 43)
HOT SPICE CAKE WITH BUTTERSCOTCH SAUCE   COFFEE

Baked Ham in Mustard Sauce

2½ cups diced ham
5 medium-sized white potatoes
¼ cup butter
¼ cup flour
¼ teaspoon salt
⅛ teaspoon pepper
2 teaspoons onion juice

2 tablespoons prepared
  mustard
2 cups milk
⅓ cup crushed corn flakes
2 tablespoons grated cheese
2 tablespoons melted butter

Cut ham into half-inch cubes. Pare and cut potatoes into half-inch cubes. Melt the ¼ cup butter; add flour, salt, pepper, onion juice and mustard. Add milk slowly and cook until smooth and thickened. Add ham and potatoes, and turn into greased 2-quart casserole. Blend corn flakes, cheese and butter together; sprinkle over ham mixture and bake.

French-Style Green Beans

1 package frozen French-cut green beans

2 tablespoons butter
½ cup water

Place beans, butter and water in saucepan. Cover tightly.

Spicecake

2 cups sifted flour
2½ teaspoons baking powder
1 teaspoon cinnamon
¼ teaspoon nutmeg
¼ teaspoon mace
¼ teaspoon allspice

⅛ teaspoon ginger
¾ cup chopped pecans
½ cup shortening
1 cup sugar
1 egg
1 cup milk

Sift together the flour, baking powder, cinnamon, nutmeg, mace, allspice, and ginger. Add nuts. Cream shortening and sugar; add egg and beat until light and creamy. Add sifted dry ingredients alternately with the milk. Pour into greased 9-inch-square pan.

TASTY BUTTERSCOTCH SAUCE

2 cups dark brown sugar
1 tablespoon orange juice
½ cup cream

¼ cup butter
⅛ teaspoon salt

In top of double boiler combine brown sugar, orange juice, cream, butter and salt. Cook over boiling water for 30 minutes, stirring occasionally. Serve hot.

Baking Directions

Preheat oven to moderate, 375° F. Place ham and green beans on lower shelf; on shelf directly above, place spice cake. Bake everything 1 hour. Heat rolls during last 10 minutes.

Menu 50. Braised Loin of Pork for Six
(90-MINUTE OVEN TIME)

BRAISED LOIN OF PORK   SPICY APPLESAUCE

STEAMED SWEET POTATOES   CORN KERNELS

LETTUCE HEARTS AND CHILI SAUCE DRESSING

CHILLED SHERRY FRUIT   MOLASSES COOKIES *   TEA

*(Buy these.)

Braised Loin of Pork

4-pound boned loin of pork	2 tablespoons butter
2 teaspoons salt	1 small onion, sliced thin
¼ teaspoon pepper	3 cups milk

Trim excess fat from pork and wipe with damp cloth. Rub well with salt and pepper; brown well in butter in Dutch oven. Add onion slices and milk; cover tightly.

Spicy Applesauce

4 cups thinly-sliced apples	1 tablespoon butter
¼ cup water	½ cup sugar
¼ cup red cinnamon candies	

Place apples in 2-quart casserole; add water, sprinkle with red candies and dot with butter. Do not cover. When removed from oven, add sugar and stir thoroughly; serve hot.

Steamed Sweet Potatoes

6 medium-sized sweet potatoes	¼ teaspoon pepper
½ cup water	3 tablespoons butter
½ teaspoon salt	

Wash, pare and cut sweet potatoes in ½-inch slices. Place in casserole with water and cover tightly. Before serving, drain and mash with remaining ingredients.

Corn Kernels

2 packages frozen whole-
kernel corn
½ cup water

1 teaspoon salt
1 teaspoon sugar
2 tablespoons melted butter

Place frozen corn in 1-quart casserole with water, salt and sugar.
Before serving, drain and toss well in melted butter.

Baking Directions

Preheat oven to moderate 375° F. Place pork on lower shelf. At
the end of 45 minutes, set sweet potatoes on shelf with pork and
place corn and applesauce on shelf directly above. Continue baking 45 minutes longer. Total oven time 90 minutes.

Tasty Extras: Lettuce Hearts and Chili Sauce Dressing

1 cup mayonnaise
4 tablespoons chili sauce
1 tablespoon chopped onion
2 tablespoons catsup
1 teaspoon vinegar
1 tablespoon chopped green
pepper

3 tablespoons chopped pimento
1 tablespoon chopped ripe
olives
1 teaspoon paprika
Lettuce hearts

Combine all ingredients and pour over lettuce hearts.

Chilled Sherry Fruit

3½ cups (No. 2½ can) mixed
fruit, drained
¼ cup of drained juice

½ cup sherry wine
½ cup cream, whipped
6 maraschino cherries

Combine drained fruit, fruit juice and sherry wine; chill in
freezer for 1 hour. Top chilled fruit with whipped cream and
garnish with cherries.

Menu 51. Roast Pork Loin for Four
(2½-HOUR OVEN TIME)

ROAST LOIN OF PORK   CATSUP APPLES

PICKLED BEETS AND ONIONS

SWEET POTATOES AU GRATIN   CORN ON THE COB

WHOLE-WHEAT BREAD *   BUTTER

PINEAPPLE SHERBET   PACKAGE-MIX WHITE CAKE

COFFEE

*(Buy this.)

Roast Loin of Pork

4-pound loin of pork
2 tablespoons flour
¼ teaspoon salt
⅛ teaspoon pepper

⅛ teaspoon rosemary
¼ teaspoon dry mustard
1 cup white wine

Wipe meat with damp cloth. Blend together flour, salt, pepper, rosemary and mustard. Rub well into meat. Place, fat side up, in roasting pan. Baste with wine after 1 hour of baking.

Catsup Apples

2 large red apples
¼ cup brown sugar

¼ cup catsup
1 cup water

Wash apples, core and cut in half through the center. Place, skin-side down, in baking pan. Top with sugar and catsup. Pour water around apples.

Sweet Potatoes au Gratin

5 medium-sized sweet
    potatoes
Water to cover
¼ cup light brown sugar
½ teaspoon salt

⅛ teaspoon pepper
2 tablespoons butter
½ cup cracker crumbs
3 tablespoons butter

Boil sweet potatoes in water to cover for 10 minutes. Peel and cut in ¼-inch slices. Place a layer of sweet potatoes in greased 1-quart casserole. Sprinkle with half of the sugar, salt and pepper. Lightly brown crumbs in 2 tablespoons of butter. Sprinkle half of the crumbs over potatoes. Repeat with second layer of potatoes, seasonings and crumbs. Dot with the 3 tablespoons butter.

Package-Mix White Cake

1 package white cake mix
¼ cup confectioners' sugar
¼ teaspoon nutmeg

Follow package directions for mixing. Pour into greased loaf pan. Before serving sprinkle with sugar mixed with nutmeg.

Baking Directions

Preheat oven to moderate, 350° F. Place pork on lower shelf. At the end of 1 hour baste pork with wine. Add pan of white cake. Bake 45 minutes longer. Remove cake. Baste again. Then on shelf directly above, place sweet potatoes and catsup apples. Bake 45 minutes longer. Total oven time 2½ hours.

Tempting Dessert: Pineapple Sherbet

⅔ cup sugar
½ cup pineapple juice
½ teaspoon grated lemon rind
1 tablespoon lemon juice
2 cups light cream or evaporated milk
2 egg whites

Combine sugar, pineapple juice, lemon rind and lemon juice. Stir until sugar is dissolved. Add milk. Pour into refrigerator tray and freeze firm, about 2 hours. Remove to cold bowl and beat until creamy. Fold in beaten egg whites. Return to refrigerator and freeze until firm, about 1½ hours.

Menu 52. Tipsy Pig for Six
(90-MINUTE OVEN TIME)

TIPSY PIG

CORN-AND-POTATO CASSEROLE

CRANBERRY-PECAN SALAD WITH CREAM CHEESE DRESSING

ORANGE SHERBET *   CHOCOLATE WAFERS *

COFFEE

*(Buy these.)

Tipsy Pig

2 cloves garlic
2 tablespoons olive oil
3 pounds pork steak
¼ teaspoon basil

¼ cup chopped parsley
2 tablespoons chopped green
    pepper
1 cup red wine

Brown garlic in olive oil. Remove garlic. Brown meat quickly in oil; place in 9- by 12-inch baking pan. Add basil, parsley, green pepper and half of the wine. Cover tightly. 15 minutes before serving, stir in remaining wine and bake uncovered.

Corn-and-Potato Casserole

¼ pound bacon
1 small onion, chopped fine
½ teaspoon salt
1 teaspoon celery salt

4 large cold boiled potatoes
1 cup (8-oz. can) creamed-
    style corn
2 tablespoons milk

Cut bacon into small pieces and fry until golden. Drain; mix with onion, salt and celery salt. Cube potatoes. Arrange potatoes and bacon in layers in buttered baking dish. Thin corn with milk and pour over bacon and potatoes.

Baking Directions

Preheat to moderate, 350° F. Place pork on lower shelf. Bake 50 minutes. Then place corn-and-potato casserole on shelf directly above the pork. Bake 40 minutes longer. Total oven time 90 minutes.

Cranberry Pecan Salad

2¼ cups sugar
½ cup water
1 pound cranberries
1½ tablespoons gelatine

¼ cup cold water
¾ cup chopped pecans
¾ cup chopped celery
Lettuce leaves

Boil sugar and water together for 5 minutes. Add cranberries and cook slowly, without stirring, for 5 minutes or until all the skins pop. Soften gelatine in cold water. Strain cranberries and mash pulp well. Combine with strained juice. Add gelatine. Let cool. When mixture begins to set, fold in chopped pecans and celery. Chill until firm. Serve on lettuce leaf with cream-cheese dressing.

CREAM-CHEESE DRESSING

3-ounce package cream cheese
2 teaspoons sugar

½ teaspoon vanilla
2 tablespoons milk

Allow cheese to soften at room temperature. Cream with fork, adding sugar, vanilla and milk. Beat until fluffy.

Menu 53. Pork Steak and Rice for Four

(75-MINUTE OVEN TIME)

PORK STEAK AND RICE   MUSTARD PICKLES

TINY WHOLE CARROTS   PEARL ONIONS

CRANBERRY-NUT BREAD   BUTTER

DEEP-DISH BLUEBERRY PIE WITH ORANGE HARD SAUCE (MENU 29)

COFFEE

Pork Steak and Rice

1½ pounds pork steak
4 cups boiled rice
8 small whole carrots
3½ cups (No. 2½ can) pearl onions

1¾ cups hot water
1 teaspoon salt
¼ teaspoon pepper
2 ripe tomatoes

Cut ¾-inch thick pork steak into 4 serving pieces. In greased 2½-quart casserole place boiled rice, whole carrots and drained onions. Combine water and salt. Pour over vegetables. Sprinkle with pepper. Arrange portions of steak on top of vegetables. Cover each portion with ½ tomato. Do not cover.

Cranberry-Nut Bread

2 cups sifted all-purpose flour
½ teaspoon salt
2 teaspoons baking powder
½ teaspoon baking soda
1 cup sugar
1 orange, grated rind and juice

2 tablespoons melted shortening
Boiling water
1 egg
1 cup chopped raw cranberries
1 cup coarsely chopped nuts

Sift together flour, salt, baking powder, soda and sugar. Add orange rind. Place orange juice and melted shortening in measuring cup and add boiling water to make ¾ cup. Beat egg; add to liquid and stir into dry ingredients. Fold in nuts and cranberries. Pour batter into well-greased loaf pan.

Deep-Dish Blueberry Pie

¼ cup boiling water
½ cup shortening
1½ cups all-purpose flour
½ teaspoon baking soda
1 quart blueberries
1 cup sugar

¼ cup all-purpose flour
⅛ teaspoons salt
1 tablespoon lemon juice
1 tablespoon cream
1 teaspoon sugar

Pour boiling water over shortening. Beat until creamy. Add flour and ½ teaspoon salt and mix to a soft dough with a fork. Wrap in wax paper and chill. Pick over blueberries, removing stems and imperfect berries. Wash and drain. Mix together sugar, flour and ⅛ teaspoon salt; add drained blueberries and toss until all are sugared. Pour into greased 9-inch-square baking pan. Sprinkle with lemon juice. Roll chilled pastry ¼-inch thick and cover blueberries to ½ inch beyond edge of pan. Flute pastry to edge of pan. Cut steam vents. Brush with cream and sprinkle with sugar.

Baking Directions

Preheat oven to moderate, 350° F. Place pork on lower shelf. On shelf directly above, place cranberry bread and blueberry pie. After 50 minutes baking time, remove pie and bake 25 minutes longer. Total oven time 75 minutes.

Menu 54. Individual Pork Roasts for Six

(75-MINUTE OVEN TIME)

INDIVIDUAL PORK ROASTS

CANDIED SWEET POTATOES   BUTTERED BABY LIMA BEANS

FRENCH BREAD *   BUTTER

TOSSED SALAD WITH ROQUEFORT DRESSING

CINNAMON APPLE ROLL WITH NUTMEG SAUCE   COFFEE

*(Buy this.)

Individual Pork Roasts

6 double pork chops
2 cups fine soft bread crumbs
¼ cup melted butter
1 small onion, diced fine
¼ teaspoon salt
⅛ teaspoon pepper

⅛ teaspoon orégano
½ teaspoon crushed sage
1½ cups water
¼ cup chili sauce
¼ teaspoon Worcestershire
 sauce

Wipe chops with damp cloth. Cut pocket in meaty side of each. Make a stuffing of bread crumbs, butter, onion, salt, pepper, orégano and sage. Stuff chop pockets with dressing. Brown stuffed chops on both sides. Place in 9- by 12-inch baking pan. Mix together water, chili sauce and Worcestershire sauce and pour over chops.

Candied Sweet Potatoes

6 large cooked sweet potatoes
1 cup brown sugar

½ teaspoon salt
⅓ cup melted butter

Peel boiled sweet potatoes. Cut in ½-inch slices. Into greased casserole place layers of potatoes sprinkled with sugar and salt. Repeat until all potatoes are used. Pour melted butter over potatoes. Cover tightly.

Buttered Baby Lima Beans

2 packages frozen baby Lima
 beans
½ cup water

2 tablespoons butter
¼ teaspoon salt
⅛ teaspoon pepper

Place beans and water in saucepan. Cover tightly. Before serving, drain and season with butter, salt, and pepper.

Cinnamon Apple Roll

1½ cups sugar
½ teaspoon nutmeg
2 cups water
2 tablespoons butter
2 cups sifted flour
4 teaspoons baking powder
1½ tablespoons sugar
½ teaspoon salt

⅓ cup shortening
⅔ cup milk
2½ cups chopped apples
½ cup sugar
2 teaspoons cinnamon
1 teaspoon grated lemon rind
2 tablespoons soft butter

Mix together sugar, nutmeg and water and add butter. Boil for 5 minutes. Sift together flour, baking powder, sugar and salt. Cut in shortening. Add milk to form dough. Roll out into long rectangle. Cover with apples. Mix together sugar, cinnamon and lemon rind and sift over apples. Dot with butter. Roll lengthwise; cut into 1-inch slices. Place, cut-side up, in greased 9-inch square pan. Pour over *half* of the hot sirup. Reserve remaining sirup to serve hot with the apple roll.

Baking Directions

Preheat oven to moderate, 375° F. Place beans and potatoes on lower shelf. On shelf directly above, set pork and apple roll. Bake 75 minutes.

Piquant Touch: Tossed Salad with Roquefort Dressing

3 cups torn, not cut, salad
   greens
⅓ cup French dressing

2 tablespoons Roquefort (or
   blue) cheese
¼ teaspoon onion juice

Combine last three ingredients and coat greens with them.
Note: To serve four, use 2 cups of greens, ¼ cup of French dressing, and reduce remaining two ingredients slightly.

Menu 55. Breaded Pork Chops for Four

(60-MINUTE OVEN TIME)

BREADED PORK CHOPS   SPICY APPLESAUCE (MENU 50)

SCALLOPED POTATOES AND ONIONS   BUTTERED CARROTS

POPPYSEED ROLLS *   BUTTER

BAKED RHUBARB   LEMON COOKIES *   COFFEE

*(Buy these.)

Baked Pork Chops

4 inch-thick pork chops
1/4 cup flour
1/2 teaspoon salt
1/8 teaspoon pepper
1/4 teaspoon paprika
1 egg
1 tablespoon water
1/2 cup bread crumbs

1/3 cup fat
2 tablespoons flour
1 1/4 cups water
1/4 teaspoon Worcestershire sauce
1/3 cup catsup
1/16 teaspoon garlic sauce
1/4 teaspoon salt

Wipe pork chops. Blend flour, salt, pepper and paprika. Flour chops and dip in egg beaten with water. Dip into crumbs. Brown in hot fat. Remove chops. Add 2 tablespoons flour, water, Worcestershire sauce, seasonings. Blend well and simmer for 2 minutes. Pour half of the sauce into greased 2-quart casserole. Place chops on sauce and pour over remaining sauce.

Scalloped Potatoes and Onions

6 medium potatoes
2 large onions
1/4 cup butter
1/4 cup flour

1/2 teaspoon dry mustard
1/2 teaspoon salt
1/4 teaspoon pepper
2 cups milk

Pare and slice potatoes ¼-inch thick. Place in ice water. Peel and slice onions ¼-inch thick. Melt butter; add flour, mustard, salt and pepper. Stir smooth. Add milk and cook until thickened, stirring constantly. Drain potatoes. Into greased casserole place alternate layers of potatoes and onions. Cover with prepared sauce.

Buttered Carrots

8 carrots
½ cup water
¼ teaspoon salt

½ teaspoon sugar
2 tablespoons butter
⅛ teaspoon pepper

Scrape carrots. Cut into thirds and place in saucepan with water, salt and sugar. Cover tightly. Before serving, drain and season with butter and pepper.

Baked Rhubarb

4 cups rhubarb, cut in 1-inch
    pieces

1⅓ cups sugar
¼ cup water

Into greased 1½-quart casserole place rhubarb. Sprinkle with sugar; add water and cover.

Baking Directions

Preheat oven to moderate, 350° F. Place carrots, applesauce and rhubarb on lower shelf. On shelf directly above, place pork chops and potatoes. Bake 60 minutes.

Menu 56. Corn-Stuffed Pork Chops for Six

(90-MINUTE OVEN TIME)

CORN-STUFFED PORK CHOPS

APPLESAUCE SALAD (MENU 43)

CANDIED ACORN SQUASH   FRENCH FRIED ONION RINGS

CINNAMON BUNS *   BUTTER

LEMON DESSERT WITH COCONUT   COFFEE

*(Buy these.)

Corn-Stuffed Pork Chops

6 inch-thick pork chops
2 cups zwieback crumbs
½ cup cream-style corn
1 egg
1 teaspoon salt

2 tablespoons chopped green
   pepper
1 tablespoon onion juice
2 tablespoons butter, melted

Put pork chops in baking pan with about ½-inch water. Mix crumbs with corn. Add slightly beaten egg, salt, green pepper, onion juice and butter. Divide into 6 portions. Cover each pork chop with dressing.

Candied Acorn Squash

4 acorn squash
Cold water to cover
¼ teaspoon salt

⅛ teaspoon pepper
1 cup dark brown sugar
3 tablespoons butter, melted

Wash squash. Cover with cold water and bring to boil. Boil 5 minutes. Drain and peel squash; slice into thirds, removing seeds. Place in greased 9-inch-square pan. Sprinkle with salt and pepper. Cover with brown sugar mixed with melted butter.

French Fried Onion Rings

2 packages frozen onion rings   ¼ teaspoon salt

Spread out frozen onions in baking pan. Sprinkle with salt before serving.

Lemon Dessert with Coconut

¾ cup sugar
3 tablespoons butter
2 eggs, separated
3 tablespoons flour

1 lemon, grated rind and juice
1 cup milk
½ cup coconut

Cream sugar and butter together; add well-beaten egg yolks. Add flour and lemon rind and juice. Add milk slowly, beating until smooth. Fold in stiffly-beaten egg whites. Pour into greased 8-inch baking dish. Set in pan of hot water. Top with coconut last 15 minutes of baking.

Baking Directions

Preheat oven to moderate, 350° F. Place chops on lower shelf; on shelf directly above, set pudding. After 50 minutes, remove pudding and place squash and onion rings on top shelf. Baste chops and bake 40 minutes longer. Heat cinnamon buns in last 10 minutes. Total oven time 90 minutes.

Menu 57. Casserole of Pork Chops for Four

(60-MINUTE OVEN TIME)

TOMATO JUICE   CHEESE CRACKERS
CASSEROLE OF PORK CHOPS
SWEET POTATO IN ORANGE BASKETS   SPICY LIMA BEANS
PINEAPPLE COLESLAW (MENU 25)
HOT APPLESAUCE CAKE WITH APPLE-BRANDY TOPPING   COFFEE

Casserole of Pork Chops

4 loin pork chops
⅓ cup chopped onion
3 tablespoons chopped celery
2 tablespoons chopped green
    pepper

½ teaspoon salt
¼ teaspoon pepper
⅛ teaspoon garlic salt
1 cup water
⅓ cup catsup

Brown chops lightly on both sides in heavy pan on top of stove. Place them in large casserole and add remaining ingredients. Cover tightly.

Sweet Potato in Orange Baskets

2 cups mashed sweet potatoes
3 tablespoons butter
¼ teaspoon salt

⅛ teaspoon pepper
2 oranges
2 marshmallows, cut in half

Combine mashed sweet potatoes with butter, salt and pepper. Place in top of double boiler to keep warm. Cut oranges in half and remove most of the orange pulp, leaving very little in the orange-skin cup. Fill each with sweet potato mixture and top with half a marshmallow. Place in 8-inch baking pan.

Spicy Lima Beans

½ cup diced bacon
½ cup chopped onion
2 tablespoons flour
¼ teaspoon salt
⅛ teaspoon pepper

1 bay leaf
1½ cups cooked tomatoes
2 cups cooked Lima beans
½ cup fine bread crumbs
3 tablespoons melted butter

Brown bacon and onion in large frying pan; add flour, salt, pepper and bay leaf, and stir until smooth. Add tomatoes and Lima beans, blend well and pour into greased 2-quart casserole dish. Combine fine crumbs and melted butter, and sprinkle over top of casserole.

Hot Applesauce Cake

½ cup shortening
1½ cups sugar
2 eggs, beaten
1 cup thick unsweetened apple-
    sauce
2 cups sifted all-purpose flour

¼ teaspoon salt
1 teaspoon baking powder
½ teaspoon baking soda
1 teaspoon cinnamon
½ teaspoon ground cloves
1 cup raisins

Cream shortening and sugar; add eggs and applesauce. Sift together flour, salt, baking powder, baking soda, cinnamon and cloves, and add to first mixture a little at a time, blending well after each addition. Stir in raisins and pour into greased 9-inch-square baking pan.

APPLE-BRANDY TOPPING

¼ cup butter
2 cups confectioners sugar,
    sifted

½ teaspoon brandy flavoring
⅓ cup hot applesauce

Blend ingredients together in order listed above. Serve one tablespoon of this mixture on each portion of hot applesauce cake.

Baking Directions

Preheat oven to moderate, 350° F. Place pork chops on lower shelf, and set cake at back of shelf directly above. At the end of 30 minutes baking time, place Lima beans on shelf with pork chops and orange baskets on shelf with cake. Continue baking 30 minutes longer. Total baking time 60 minutes.

Menu 58. Spareribs and Sauerkraut for Four

(65-MINUTE OVEN TIME)

SPARERIBS AND SAUERKRAUT

OVEN-BOILED POTATOES   OVEN-COOKED PEAS

DARK RYE BREAD   BUTTER

HOT GINGERBREAD WITH VANILLA ICE CREAM   COFFEE

Spareribs and Sauerkraut

3 pounds spareribs, cut in serving pieces
1½ cups water
1 teaspoon salt

4 cups (No. 3 can) sauerkraut
1 teaspoon caraway seeds
2 apples, pared and chopped
2 onions, chopped

Combine spareribs, water and salt and steam 20 minutes. Blend sauerkraut, caraway seeds, chopped apple and chopped onion, and place in 9 by 14 inch greased baking pan. Place steamed spareribs on top.

Oven-Boiled Potatoes

8 small potatoes
1 cup water

¼ teaspoon salt

Pare potatoes; place in saucepan and add water and salt and cover tightly.

Oven-Cooked Peas

3 tablespoons butter
2 tablespoons water

1 package frozen peas

Place butter, water and frozen peas in casserole and cover tightly.

Hot Gingerbread

½ cup sugar
1 cup cake flour
¼ teaspoon cinnamon
¼ teaspoon mace
¼ teaspoon allspice
¼ teaspoon cloves
½ teaspoon ginger

½ teaspoon salt
1 egg, beaten
¼ cup molasses
¼ cup shortening, melted
1 teaspoon soda
½ cup boiling water
1 teaspoon vanilla

Sift together sugar, flour, cinnamon, mace, allspice, cloves, ginger and salt. Blend beaten egg, molasses and melted shortening; add to sifted dry ingredients and stir until smooth. Combine baking soda and boiling water; add to first mixture with vanilla and stir until well blended. Pour the thin batter into a greased, 8-inch-square cake pan.

Baking Directions

Preheat oven to moderate, 375° F. Place spareribs and sauerkraut on lower shelf. At the end of 30 minutes, set potatoes on lowest shelf with spareribs, and on the shelf directly above place the peas and gingerbread. Continue baking for 35 minutes longer, 65 minutes in all.

Menu 59. Sunday Breakfast for Four
(50-MINUTE OVEN TIME)

BAKED APPLES

SAUSAGE CAKES AND BACON

POPOVERS   BUTTER   RASPBERRY JAM   COFFEE

(DRIED FRUIT COMPOTE FOR TOMORROW)

Baked Apples

4 firm apples
1 cup white sugar
1 cup water
4 tablespoons brown sugar

1 teaspoon cinnamon
1 tablespoon butter
1 tablespoon white sugar

Core apples, pare top half of each and place in greased 2½-quart casserole. Combine the 1 cup of white sugar and 1 cup of water and boil for 3 minutes. In each apple place 1 tablespoon brown sugar, sprinkle with cinnamon and dot with butter. Sprinkle the remaining 1 tablespoon of white sugar over the top of the apples. Pour the sugar sirup around base of apples.

Sausage Cakes and Bacon

1 pound ground sausage meat   4 strips bacon
½ cup fine bread crumbs

Blend sausage meat and bread crumbs. Shape into 4 large flat cakes. Wrap each with a strip of bacon and secure with a toothpick. Place in shallow 8-inch baking pan.

Popovers

1¼ cups sifted all-purpose flour | 2 eggs
¼ teaspoon salt | 1 cup milk
1 teaspoon sugar | 1 tablespoon butter, melted

Sift together flour, salt and sugar. Combine eggs and milk and beat well. Pour egg mixture over sifted dry ingredients and beat with egg beater until smooth. Stir in melted butter and continue beating for 2 *minutes*. Fill greased muffin pans ⅔ full.

Baking Directions

Preheat oven to hot, 400° F. Place pans containing apples and sausage cakes on lower shelf. Place popovers in center of shelf directly above. Bake 50 minutes at 400° F.

Note: Prick each popover with point of sharp knife 3 minutes before removing from oven. This will increase crispness.

Dried Fruit Compote

8 prunes | 1 quart cold water
8 apricots | ¾ cup sugar
8 peaches | ¼ cup sherry wine

Wash fruit. Place in 2½-quart casserole and add remaining ingredients. Cover. Place in hot oven immediately after breakfast is removed. Turn heat off. Let stand in oven 4 hours. Chill before serving.

Note: Dried fruits prepared in this way do not require soaking.

Menu 60. Holiday Breakfast for Four

(60-MINUTE OVEN TIME)

CHILLED ORANGE JUICE

WHOLE-WHEAT CEREAL   CREAM AND SUGAR

SHIRRED EGGS   CRISP BACON

HOT MUFFINS   BUTTER   STRAWBERRY JAM   COFFEE

Whole-Wheat Cereal

Follow package directions as to amount of cereal, salt and water.
Place in saucepan; cover tightly. Before serving, beat to remove
any lumps.

Note: A quick-cooking type of cereal should be used.

Shirred Eggs

¼ cup heavy cream   4 eggs
4 teaspoons butter   ¼ teaspoon salt
¼ cup catsup   ⅛ teaspoon pepper
4 drops Tabasco sauce

Grease 4 individual custard cups. Into each cup place 1 tablespoon cream, 1 teaspoon butter, 1 tablespoon catsup and 1 drop
Tabasco sauce. Break 1 egg into each cup. Sprinkle with salt and
pepper.

Variation: Place a thin slice of sharp cheese over each egg.

Crisp Bacon

½ pound bacon

Do not separate bacon. Place, in one piece, in shallow baking pan.

Hot Muffins

2 cups sifted flour
½ teaspoon salt
3 teaspoons baking powder
2 tablespoons sugar

1 egg, beaten
1 cup milk
2 tablespoons melted butter

Sift together flour, salt, baking powder and sugar. Beat egg and add milk. Add liquids to sifted dry ingredients; stir slightly, add melted butter and mix. Do not beat. Batter should be lumpy. Fill 12 greased muffin tins ⅔ full.
Variation: For *Surprise Muffins,* add 1 cup pitted chopped dates, or ½ cup seedless raisins, or 1 cup blueberries after batter is mixed.

Baking Directions

Preheat oven to hot, 400° F. Place cereal and bacon on lower shelf. After 35 minutes, place eggs and muffins on upper shelf. Bake 25 minutes longer. Total oven time 60 minutes.

Menu 61. Easy Sausage Supper for Eight
(45-MINUTE OVEN TIME)

SAUSAGE-RICE

MARINATED VEGETABLES

CRISP SALAD GREENS WITH CUCUMBER SOUR-CREAM DRESSING

ICE CREAM PUFFS WITH STRAWBERRIES   MOCHA COFFEE

Sausage-Rice

2 cups raw rice
4 quarts boiling water
2 tablespoons salt
3 green peppers
3 medium-sized onions
¼ cup butter

2 pounds link sausages
3½ cups (No. 2½ can) solid-
  pack tomatoes
¼ teaspoon basil
½ teaspoon salt

Wash rice in cold water. Add to boiling salted water and boil until tender, about 25 minutes. Wash peppers, remove seeds and membrane, and chop. Peel and chop onions. Simmer peppers and onions in butter until tender. Add to drained rice. Coarsely chop half the sausages and fry for 10 minutes. Add to rice with tried-out fat. Crush tomatoes and add with basil and ½ teaspoon of the salt to rice. Blend together rice, simmered onions and peppers, fried chopped sausages and tomatoes. Turn into 9- by 14-inch greased pan. Arrange remaining whole link sausages on top.

Ice Cream Puffs

⅓ cup butter
¾ cup boiling water
¾ cup flour

¼ teaspoon salt
3 eggs

Melt butter; add water and bring to a boil. Add flour and salt, all at once, at the range, and stir vigorously. Mixture will form a ball which doesn't separate. Remove from heat and cool for 10 minutes. Add eggs, one at a time, beating hard after each addition. Mixture will become smooth. Drop into 8 mounds on greased cooky sheet and bake.

Allow cream puffs to cool. Split half way around bottom with sharp knife. Fill with vanilla ice cream and top with sugared fresh or frozen strawberries.

Baking Directions

Preheat oven to hot, 400° F. Place sausage-rice on lower shelf. On shelf directly above, place cream puffs. Bake both 45 minutes.

Perfect Extra: Mocha Coffee

Add 1 tablespoon instant cocoa to regular-grind coffee. Make in usual way.

Crisp Salad Greens with Cucumber Sour-Cream Dressing

1 pint sour cream
1½ cups finely chopped cucumber
2 tablespoons grated onion
1 tablespoon prepared mustard

3 tablespoons tarragon vinegar
1½ teaspoons sugar
½ teaspoon salt
¼ teaspoon pepper
6 cups crisp salad greens

Blend all ingredients together; chill before serving over greens

Menu 62. Veal in Sherry for Four
(60-MINUTE OVEN TIME)

VEAL CUTLET IN SHERRY SAUCE

WHIPPED POTATOES   DUTCH ASPARAGUS

CABBAGE FRUIT MOLD (MENU 15)   FRENCH BREAD *   BUTTER

PINEAPPLE COCONUT SQUARES   COFFEE

*(Buy this.)

Veal Cutlet in Sherry Sauce

1½ pounds veal cutlet, cut in
    serving portions
2 tablespoons flour
½ teaspoon salt
½ teaspoon paprika
2 tablespoons fat

1 onion, thinly sliced
1 can condensed mushroom
    soup
¼ cup water
¼ cup sherry wine

Wipe cutlet with damp cloth. Mix flour, salt and paprika together and rub into cutlet. Brown on both sides in hot fat. Place browned cutlet in greased 2-quart casserole. Cover with very thinly-sliced onions. Blend soup, water and wine. Pour over onions. Cover tightly.

Whipped Potatoes

5 medium-sized potatoes
½ cup water
¼ teaspoon salt

⅛ teaspoon pepper
2 tablespoons butter
2 tablespoons hot milk

Wash and pare potatoes. Cut into quarters. Place in saucepan with water. Cover tightly. Before serving, mash, season with salt, pepper and butter; add milk and whip with fork.

Dutch Asparagus

1 No. 2 can all-green asparagus
2 tablespoons butter
2 tablespoons flour
¼ teaspoon salt
⅛ teaspoon pepper
⅛ teaspoon dry mustard

1 cup milk
½ cup soft sharp cheese
½ cup dry bread crumbs
¼ cup melted butter
1 pimento, cut in strips

Drain asparagus. Place in greased 8-inch baking pan. Melt 2 tablespoons butter; add flour, salt, pepper and mustard. Stir until smooth; add milk slowly. Add cheese and cook until smooth and thickened. Pour over asparagus. Combine crumbs and ¼ cup melted butter. Sprinkle over sauce and asparagus. Top with pimento strips.

Pineapple Coconut Squares

1 cup sifted all-purpose flour
¼ teaspoon salt
1 tablespoon sugar
2 teaspoons baking powder
1½ tablespoons butter
3 eggs

1 cup drained crushed pine-apple
1 cup sugar
1 tablespoon melted butter
2 cups moist shredded coconut

Sift together flour, salt, 1 tablespoon sugar and baking powder. Cut in 1½ tablespoons butter. Beat eggs thoroughly. Add half of the beaten-egg mixture to flour mixture and mix well. Pour into greased 8-inch-square pan. Sprinkle with pineapple. Mix together 1 cup sugar, melted butter, coconut and remaining egg mixture. Spread over pineapple.

Baking Directions

Preheat oven to moderate, 350° F. Place veal and potatoes on lower shelf. On shelf directly above, place pineapple squares. At the end of 40 minutes, remove pineapple squares and place asparagus on upper shelf. Bake 20 minutes longer. Total oven time 60 minutes.

Menu 63. Veal Party Fare for Six
(80-MINUTE OVEN TIME)

VEAL MARINADE WITH MUSHROOMS

PICKLES, CELERY AND OLIVES

BROWNED POTATOES   MINTED WHOLE CARROTS

HOT ROLLS *   BUTTER

ORANGE MERINGUE PUDDING   COFFEE

*(Buy these.)

Veal Marinade with Mushrooms

2 pounds veal steak, cut ¾ inch thick
⅓ cup wine vinegar
⅓ cup dry red wine
1 onion, sliced

1 clove garlic
1 bay leaf
6 whole cloves
3 tablespoons olive oil

Cut veal into serving pieces. Mix together vinegar, wine, sliced onion, crushed clove of garlic, bay leaf, cloves and oil. Pour over veal and refrigerate, covered, overnight.

3 tablespoons shortening
½ pound mushrooms, sliced
1 medium-sized onion, sliced

½ cup red wine
1 teaspoon salt
½ teaspoon pepper

Remove veal from marinade. Dry on paper towels. Brown on both sides in hot fat. Remove veal to greased 9-by-12-inch baking pan. Add sliced mushrooms and onions. Add wine to pan juices. Add salt and pepper and pour over veal. Cover.

Browned Potatoes

12 small new potatoes
1 cup water

½ teaspoon salt
¼ cup shortening, melted

Wash potatoes; place in saucepan with water and salt. When almost cooked, peel. Dip into melted shortening and place in baking pan with remaining shortening to brown.

Minted Carrots

18 small carrots
1 cup water
½ teaspoon salt

¼ cup butter
2 tablespoons chopped fresh
   mint

Scrape carrots. Place in saucepan with water and salt. Cover tightly. Before serving, season with butter and mint.

Orange Meringue Pudding

2 egg yolks
¼ cup sugar
¼ teaspoon salt
2 tablespoons butter, melted
2 teaspoons grated orange rind
1 teaspoon grated lemon rind

1 cup orange juice
1 cup milk
3 cups day-old bread cubes
½ cup seedless raisins
½ cup pecans

Beat egg yolks; add sugar, salt, butter, orange rind, lemon rind, orange juice and milk. Pour over bread cubes. Add raisins and pecans. Pour into greased loaf pan.

MERINGUE

2 egg whites
2 tablespoons cold water

¼ cup sugar
1 orange, peeled and sliced

Beat egg whites and water until stiff. Add sugar slowly and beat until very stiff. Cover partially-baked pudding with meringue, decorate with orange slices and return to oven to complete baking.

Baking Directions

Preheat oven to moderate, 350° F. Place veal and potatoes on lower shelf. On shelf directly above, set carrots and pudding. At the end of 40 minutes, remove potatoes; peel, grease and return to oven to brown. Remove pudding after 1 hour baking time. Top with meringue and return to oven for 20 minutes. Place rolls in oven to heat for last 10 minutes. Total oven time 80 minutes.

Menu 64. Rolled Veal Dinner for Eight
(4-HOUR OVEN TIME)

ROLLED VEAL CUTLET

VEGETABLE CASSEROLE

BREAD STICKS *   BUTTER

LETTUCE HEARTS AND CHILI SAUCE DRESSING (MENU 50)

APPLE PIE   SNAPPY CHEESE   COFFEE

*(Buy these.)

Rolled Veal Cutlet

3 tablespoons grated lemon
     rind
½ teaspoon salt
¼ teaspoon pepper
6 pounds sliced veal cutlet, cut
     ½-inch thick
¼ pound sliced bacon

2 hard-cooked eggs
1 cup dry bread crumbs
½ teaspoon sage
1 tablespoon onion, finely
     chopped
½ cup water
1 can chicken bouillon

Sprinkle lemon rind, salt and pepper over veal. Arrange bacon and sliced eggs over veal. Top with dressing made by blending bread crumbs, sage, onion and water. Roll up meat and tie or fasten with skewers; place in baking pan.

Vegetable Casserole

8 medium-sized potatoes
8 tomatoes
¼ cup butter
¼ cup flour
1 teaspoon salt

¼ teaspoon pepper
¼ teaspoon mustard
2 cups milk
3 medium-sized onions

Pare and slice potatoes ¼ inch thick. Slice tomatoes ⅓ inch thick. Alternate layers of potatoes and tomatoes in 3-quart greased casserole. Make white sauce by melting butter. Add to this flour, salt, pepper and mustard. Stir until smooth; add milk and bring to a boil. Pour over potatoes and tomatoes. On top arrange thick slices of onion.

Apple Pie

2 packages pastry mix
6 tart apples
1 quart water
½ teaspoon salt
1 cup sugar
¼ teaspoon salt
2 tablespoons flour

⅛ teaspoon cinnamon
¼ teaspoon nutmeg
1½ teaspoons grated lemon
    rind
1 tablespoon butter
1 tablespoon cream

Line 10-inch pie plate with pastry. Pare, core and slice apples into water to which ½ teaspoon salt has been added. Drain. Blend together salt, sugar, flour, cinnamon, nutmeg and lemon rind. Sprinkle over the pastry 1 tablespoon of the sugar mixture. Toss remaining sugar mixture with drained apples. Pile in pie plate. Dot with butter and top with pastry, sealing edges together. Brush with cream; make slits in top crust to allow steam to escape.

Baking Directions

Preheat oven to very hot, 500° F. Place veal on lower shelf; on shelf directly above, place apple pie. At the end of 20 minutes reduce heat to 350°. Baste meat and continue baking 40 minutes longer. Remove pie and add bouillon to veal. Cover with aluminum foil. Add vegetable casserole. Bake 3 hours longer. Total oven time 4 hours.

Menu 65. Creamed Veal Birds for Six

(75-MINUTE OVEN TIME)

VEAL BIRDS

CANDIED SWEET POTATOES   SUCCOTASH

CUCUMBER SALAD   POPPYSEED ROLLS *   BUTTER

DATE-AND-NUT PUDDING   APPLE-BRANDY TOPPING (MENU 57)

TEA

(CUP CUSTARDS FOR TOMORROW)

*(Buy these.)

Veal Birds

2 pounds veal, sliced ¼ inch thick	1 teaspoon salt
	¼ teaspoon pepper
3 slices bacon, cut in half	¼ cup shortening, melted
6 thin slices onion	2 cups evaporated milk

Cut veal slices into 6 pieces, 2 inches wide and 3 inches long. Place a piece of bacon and a slice of onion on each, sprinkle with salt and pepper. Roll tightly and secure with toothpick. Brown in melted shortening, add milk and cover tightly.

Candied Sweet Potatoes

6 medium-sized sweet potatoes, cooked	¼ cup butter, melted
	⅔ cup maple sirup
2 tablespoons water	½ teaspoon salt

Peel potatoes and slice in ½-inch-thick slices. Place in greased 9-inch baking pan. Combine remaining ingredients and pour over sliced potatoes.

Succotash

2 packages frozen succotash	¼ cup water
3 tablespoons butter	½ teaspoon salt

Place all ingredients in 1½-quart casserole and cover tightly.

Date-and-Nut Pudding

¼ cup butter	1 teaspoon vanilla
½ cup brown sugar	1 cup chopped dates
½ cup tapioca	½ cup chopped walnuts
½ teaspoon salt	3 cups hot water

Cream butter and sugar, stir in remaining ingredients and blend thoroughly. Pour into greased 9-inch-square baking pan.

Cup Custards

3 eggs	2 cups hot milk
¼ teaspoon salt	1 teaspoon vanilla
¼ cup sugar	¼ teaspoon nutmeg

Beat eggs. Add salt, sugar, milk, and vanilla. Pour into 6 buttered custard cups. Sprinkle with nutmeg. Place cups in pan of warm water to bake.

Baking Directions

Preheat oven to moderate, 325° F. Place veal birds on lower shelf and custards on shelf directly above; at the end of 25 minutes set date pudding on shelf with custards. At the end of an additional 25 minutes, remove custards and place succotash on lower shelf and sweet potatoes on upper. Continue baking 25 minutes longer. Heat rolls during last 10 minutes. Total oven time 75 minutes.

Tempting Side Dish: Cucumber Salad

2 medium-sized cucumbers	1 tablespoon finely-chopped green pepper
1 teaspoon salt	
2 tablespoons finely chopped onion	½ cup sour cream
	1 tablespoon wine vinegar
	6 lettuce cups

Peel and thinly slice cucumbers, sprinkle with salt and place in refrigerator for 15 minutes. Combine onion, green pepper, sour cream and vinegar. Drain cucumbers and fold into dressing. Serve in crisp lettuce cups.

Menu 66. Veal à la Sherry for Six
(2¼-HOUR OVEN TIME)

VEAL A LA SHERRY

CELERY, OLIVES AND PICKLES

PARSLEY POTATOES   MINTED WHOLE CARROTS

LEMON-CAKE PUDDING WITH WHIPPED CREAM   COFFEE

(PACKAGE-MIX GINGERBREAD FOR TOMORROW)

Veal à la Sherry

½ cup olive oil
4-pound leg of veal
2 medium-sized onions, sliced
2 stalks celery, cut in 2-inch
   pieces
3 sprigs parsley
¼ cup butter

1½ teaspoons salt
¼ teaspoon pepper
1 bouillon cube
¼ cup hot water
½ cup sherry wine
1½ tablespoons flour

Heat olive oil in Dutch oven and brown veal on all sides. Remove veal and to drippings in pan add onions, celery and parsley. Place veal on top of vegetables in 9-by 12-inch pan, spread with butter and season with salt and pepper. Dissolve bouillon cube in hot water; pour over veal and add half of the sherry wine. Cover and bake. Before serving, combine remaining sherry wine and flour; mix to a paste. Remove veal from pan, strain drippings into saucepan and stir in wine paste. Cook on top of stove until thickened, stirring constantly.

Parsley Potatoes

18 small new potatoes
1 cup water
½ teaspoon salt
3 tablespoons melted butter

2 tablespoons chopped parsley
⅛ teaspoon paprika
⅛ teaspoon pepper

Wash and scrub potatoes to remove skins. Place in 3-quart casserole with water and salt, cover tightly and bake. Before serving, roll potatoes in mixture of melted butter, parsley, paprika and pepper.

Minted Whole Carrots

12 small carrots	½ teaspoon sugar
4 fresh mint leaves	½ teaspoon salt
1 cup water	2 tablespoons butter

Wash and scrape carrots. Place in casserole dish with mint leaves, water, sugar and salt. Cover tightly and bake. Before serving, roll in melted butter.

Lemon-Cake Pudding

¼ cup butter	1 teaspoon grated lemon rind
¾ cup sugar	4 tablespoons lemon juice
3 tablespoons all-purpose flour	1 cup milk
2 eggs, separated	½ pint heavy cream, whipped

Cream butter; sift together sugar and flour, and add to creamed butter; blend thoroughly. Add beaten egg yolks, lemon rind, lemon juice and beat until light and fluffy. Stir in milk and fold in beaten egg whites. Pour into greased 8-inch-square baking pan. Serve with the whipped cream or ice cream.

Baking Directions

Preheat oven to moderate, 350° F. Place veal on lower shelf in oven. At the end of 1½ hours baking time, set potatoes on shelf with veal; place carrots and pudding on shelf directly above. Continue baking 45 minutes longer. Total baking time 2¼ hours. *Note:* A pan of gingerbread-mix can be baked during the first 1½ hours. Follow package directions for mixing and baking.

Menu 67. Braised Stuffed Veal Hearts for Four

(90-MINUTE OVEN TIME)

BRAISED STUFFED VEAL HEARTS   HORSE-RADISH DRESSING

BUTTERED GREEN BEANS   BROWN RICE

CARROT-APPLE SALAD   HOT PARKER HOUSE ROLLS *   BUTTER

APRICOT CUSTARD   COFFEE

*(Buy these.)

Stuffed Veal Hearts

4 pounds veal hearts
1 teaspoon salt
¼ teaspoon pepper
1½ cups stale bread cubes
½ teaspoon sage
¼ teaspoon thyme
1 small onion, chopped fine
1 teaspoon fresh horse-radish

¼ cup butter
1 egg, beaten
½ cup flour
¼ teaspoon salt
¼ cup shortening
1 quart water
1 clove garlic, mashed
1 medium-sized onion, sliced

Wash hearts and remove valves and arteries. Rub inside and out with salt and pepper. Make a dressing by combining bread cubes, sage, thyme, onion, horse-radish, butter and egg. Pack into hearts and close opening with cord or skewers. Dredge with blended flour and salt. Brown on all sides in hot fat. Place in greased 3-quart casserole; add water, garlic and onion. Cover.

Buttered Green Beans

2 tablespoons butter
¼ cup water

1 package frozen green beans

Place butter and water in pan; add frozen beans. Cover tightly. Season before serving.

Apricot Custard

4 canned apricot halves	⅛ teaspoon salt
4 teaspoons brown sugar	⅛ teaspoon nutmeg
2 eggs	1½ cups milk
3 tablespoons sugar	½ cup apricot juice

Grease four large custard cups; arrange an apricot half, cut-side up, in bottom of each cup. Place brown sugar in hollows. Beat eggs; add sugar, salt, nutmeg, milk and apricot juice. Pour over apricot halves. Place custard cups in pan containing 1 inch cold water.

Baking Directions

Preheat oven to slow, 300° F. Place veal hearts on lower shelf. On shelf directly above, place custards; at the end of 1 hour remove custards. Check hearts to be sure they have enough liquid. Add more water if needed. Place green beans on top shelf and bake 30 minutes longer. Add rolls for last 10 minutes of baking. Total oven time 90 minutes.

Note: Prepare salad and cook rice during last 30 minutes of oven time.

Carrot-Apple Salad

2 tart apples	2 carrots grated
2 cups cold water	⅓ cup salad dressing
½ teaspoon salt	Lettuce leaves

Pare, core, and dice apples. Place in cold salted water for 1 minute. Drain and add carrots and salad dressing. Chill and serve on lettuce leaf.

Menu 68. Sausage-Stuffed Veal for Six
(90-MINUTE OVEN TIME)

SAUSAGE-STUFFED VEAL STEAK

SWEET POTATO-ALMOND MOUNDS   BUTTERED BROCCOLI

CHILLED CUCUMBERS WITH FRENCH DRESSING   SALT STICKS *

ORANGE TORTE WITH WHIPPED CREAM   COFFEE

*(Buy these.)

Sausage-Stuffed Veal Steak

2 one-pound veal steaks, ½
   inch thick
2 tablespoons shortening
½ pound sausage meat
3 cups soft bread crumbs
¼ teaspoon basil
1 tablespoon parsley
¹⁄₁₆ teaspoon nutmeg

¼ teaspoon salt
⅛ teaspoon pepper
2 eggs, beaten
1 tablespoon lemon juice
⅓ cup applesauce
3 strips bacon
½ cup red wine
½ cup water

Brown veal in fat on both sides. Mix sausage meat, crumbs, basil, parsley, nutmeg, salt, pepper, eggs, lemon juice and applesauce. Pack on top of browned veal steak. Cover with second steak. With toothpicks fasten strips of bacon around edges to hold in dressing. Place on rack in greased 3-quart casserole, add wine and water and cover.

Sweet Potato-Almond Mounds

2 cans sweet potatoes
3 tablespoons melted butter
¼ teaspoon salt
⅛ teaspoon pepper

2 tablespoons cream
⅓ cup slivered blanched
   almonds

Mash sweet potatoes. Add butter, salt, pepper and cream and beat with fork until blended. Shape into 6 mounds in 9-inch greased baking pan. Stud with almond slivers.

Buttered Broccoli

2 packages frozen broccoli
½ cup water

¼ teaspoon salt
3 tablespoons melted butter

In saucepan place broccoli, water and salt. Cover tightly. Before serving, drain and add butter.

Orange Torte

½ cup butter
1 cup sugar
3 eggs
¼ teaspoon grated orange rind
¼ teaspoon grated lemon rind
2¼ cups sifted cake flour
1 teaspoon baking powder
½ teaspoon baking soda

¼ teaspoon salt
½ cup buttermilk
½ cup sour cream
¾ cup sugar
¼ cup orange juice
3 tablespoons lemon juice
½ pint heavy cream, whipped

Cream together butter, sugar and eggs. Add orange and lemon rind. Sift together flour, baking powder, baking soda and salt. Add alternately with buttermilk and cream to butter mixture. Pour into well greased, loose-bottom, 9-inch tube pan.

Bring to a boil the sugar, orange and lemon juice; pour slowly over hot cake immediately after taking from oven. Serve with whipped cream.

Baking Directions

Preheat oven to moderate, 350° F. Place veal on lower shelf in oven. At the end of 40 minutes baking time, place broccoli on shelf with veal, and on shelf directly above place torte and sweet potatoes. Bake 50 minutes longer. Total oven time 90 minutes.

Menu 69. Baked Bean Luncheon for Six

(7-HOUR OVEN TIME)

BAKED BEANS   CHILI SAUCE   COTTAGE HAM
BOSTON BROWN BREAD   BUTTER
CABBAGE SALAD   GREEN TOMATO PICKLES
FRESH FRUIT BOWL   FIG BARS *   TEA
(CREAMY RICE PUDDING FOR TOMORROW, MENU 27)

*(Buy these.)

Baked Beans

2 cups dry pea beans
1½ teaspoons salt
1 teaspoon dry mustard
¼ teaspoon pepper
¼ cup dark molasses

2 tablespoons brown sugar
3 cups boiling water
1 medium-sized onion
¼ pound salt pork

Pick beans over carefully, removing stones and crushed beans; wash in cold water and drain. Cover beans with fresh cold water and soak overnight. Drain, rinse and again cover with cold water, and bring to boiling point; parboil 30 minutes. Drain water off beans and place them in a 3-quart casserole. Combine salt, mustard, pepper, molasses, brown sugar and boiling water; pour over beans. Bury onion in beans; cut salt pork into small squares, but do not cut through the rind, wash in cold water and bury cut side down in the beans. Additional water may be added during baking time if needed to prevent dryness or if beans are desired quite moist.

Cottage Ham

2-pound cottage ham	1½ tablespoons cinnamon
12 whole cloves	1½ tablespoons dry mustard
3 cups all-purpose flour	1 teaspoon black pepper
¾ cup brown sugar	¼ cup vinegar
1½ tablespoons ground cloves	½ cup water

Wipe ham with damp cloth and stick with whole cloves. Blend together flour, brown sugar, ground cloves, cinnamon, mustard and pepper; add vinegar and water and stir until mixture forms a stiff dough. Roll out on floured cloth or board and wrap ham in dough. Place in greased loaf pan. When baked, remove wrapping and discard. Ham will be juicy and tender and well seasoned.

Boston Brown Bread

1 cup sifted all-purpose flour	1 egg
2 teaspoons baking soda	1 tablespoon melted butter
1 tablespoon sugar	½ cup dark molasses
1 teaspoon salt	1⅔ cups buttermilk
2 cups graham flour	1 cup chopped seeded raisins

Sift together white flour, soda, sugar and salt. Stir in graham flour. Beat egg; add butter, molasses and buttermilk, and add to flour mixture and beat until smooth. Fold in raisins and pour into greased waxed-paper-lined loaf pan.

Baking Directions

Preheat oven to slow, 300° F. Place beans on lower shelf and rice pudding on shelf directly above. At the end of 2½ hours baking, remove rice pudding and bake the beans 2 hours longer. Then place ham and brown bread on upper shelf. Continue baking 2½ hours longer. Total baking time 7 hours.

Menu 70. Baked Eggs and Potatoes for Four

(45-MINUTE OVEN TIME)

CLAM CHOWDER   OYSTER CRACKERS

BAKED EGGS AND POTATOES

STEAMED ASPARAGUS WITH MOCK HOLLANDAISE SAUCE

ROSY PEAR SALAD WITH CREAM-CHEESE DRESSING

HOT HARD ROLLS *   BUTTER

HOT HONEY SPICECAKE   COFFEE

*(Buy these.)

Baked Eggs and Potatoes

4 hot baked potatoes
½ teaspoon salt
¼ teaspoon pepper
2 tablespoons butter
4 tablespoons milk

4 eggs
¼ teaspoon salt
⅛ teaspoon pepper
½ teaspoon paprika

Remove a 2-inch square of baked skin from one side of each of the baked potatoes. Scoop out pulp and mash with ½ teaspoon salt, ¼ teaspoon pepper, butter and milk; beat well. Refill baked shells within ½ inch of the top and drop a raw egg carefully into each cavity. Sprinkle with remaining salt and pepper. Place the rest of the mashed potato pulp in pastry tube or pastry bag, and pipe around eggs. Garnish with paprika and place in greased 9-inch-square pan.

Steamed Asparagus

1 bunch asparagus
1 quart water

1 tablespoon salt

Remove all scales up to the tip of each stalk of asparagus and cut off about 1½ inches of the hard part of stem. Wash asparagus well and place in loaf pan with the water and salt; cover pan tightly with aluminum foil. Serve with mock hollandaise sauce.

MOCK HOLLANDAISE SAUCE

1 cup mayonnaise	¼ teaspoon salt
⅓ cup lemon juice	¼ teaspoon paprika

Combine all ingredients and blend well; heat in top of double boiler. Serve over asparagus.

Honey Spicecake

½ cup shortening	½ teaspoon salt
½ cup sugar	½ teaspoon allspice
½ cup honey	½ teaspoon cinnamon
1 egg, well beaten	½ teaspoon baking soda
1 cup raisins	¼ teaspoon cloves
2¼ cups sifted cake flour	1 cup buttermilk
1 teaspoon baking powder	¼ cup confectioners sugar

Cream together shortening, sugar and honey; add beaten egg and raisins. Sift together cake flour, baking powder, salt, allspice, cinnamon, baking soda and cloves, and add alternately with buttermilk to creamed mixture. Blend well and pour into greased, 8-inch-square baking pan. Serve warm sprinkled with confectioners' sugar.

Baking Directions

Preheat oven to moderate, 350° F. Place honey cake on upper shelf. At the end of 20 minutes, place potatoes and asparagus on lower shelf and continue baking 25 minutes longer. Heat rolls during last 10 minutes. Total baking time 45 minutes.

Colorful Suggestion: Rosy Pear Salad

3½ cups (No. 2½ can) pear halves	1 small head lettuce
	3-ounce package cream cheese
2 packages red cinnamon candies	1 tablespoon mayonnaise
	½ cup sliced strawberries

Drain juice from pear halves. Combine juice and red candies in saucepan and cook until candies have dissolved; add pear halves to this sirup and place in refrigerator for several hours. Place chilled pears on bed of lettuce leaves. Soften cream cheese with mayonnaise and place a spoonful in each pear half. Top with sliced strawberries.

II

INTO A COLD OVEN

Menu 71. Crab-Meat Luncheon for Six
(25-MINUTE OVEN TIME)

CRAB-MEAT CASSEROLE

RAW RELISH TRAY (MENU 31)

FRENCH FRIED POTATOES   SPINACH-AND-GREEN PEPPERS

HOT BISCUITS   BUTTER   COMB HONEY

PINEAPPLE PARFAIT   COFFEE

Crab-Meat Casserole

6 tablespoons butter
6 tablespoons flour
2 cups milk
½ teaspoon salt
¼ teaspoon pepper
½ teaspoon celery salt
⅔ cup grated American cheese

½ cup chopped green pepper
½ cup cooked mushrooms, sliced
1 cup crab meat, flaked
½ cup coarse cracker crumbs
2 tablespoons melted butter

Melt butter; stir in flour. Add milk and cook, stirring constantly until thickened. Stir in salt, pepper, celery salt, cheese, green pepper, mushrooms and flaked crab meat. Turn mixture into 1½-quart casserole. Combine cracker crumbs and butter; sprinkle over crab meat mixture.

French Fried Potatoes

2 packages frozen French fried potatoes   2 teaspoons salt

Spread out potatoes in 9-by 12-inch baking pan so they do not overlap. Sprinkle with salt before serving.

Spinach-and-Green Peppers

¼ cup chopped green pepper
1 tablespoon chopped pimento
2 tablespoons chopped onion
3 tablespoons melted butter

3 cups cooked spinach
1 teaspoon salt
2 tablespoons lemon juice

Simmer pepper, pimento and onion in butter until tender. Add spinach, salt and lemon juice. Pour into greased 1-quart casserole.

Hot Biscuits

2 cups sifted all-purpose flour
3 teaspoons baking powder
½ teaspoon salt

3 tablespoons shortening
¾ cup milk

Sift dry ingredients together, cut in shortening and add milk. Blend well with a fork, turn out on lightly-floured cloth and pat to ⅔-inch thickness. Cut with 2-inch cooky cutter and place on ungreased cooky sheet. Makes 12 biscuits.

Baking Directions

Place crab meat, spinach and potatoes on lower shelf in oven. Place biscuits on shelf directly above. Set thermostat at hot 450° F., and bake everything 25 minutes.

Delightful Dessert: Pineapple Parfait

½ cup sugar
1 tablespoon cornstarch
1 cup crushed pineapple,
    including juice

1 quart vanilla ice cream
6 mint leaves

Blend sugar, cornstarch and pineapple; cook until thickened stirring constantly. Chill sauce and serve over ice cream. Garnish with mint leaves.

Menu 72. Sunday Supper for Six
(25-MINUTE OVEN TIME)

STUFFED LOBSTER ROLLS   BREAD AND BUTTER PICKLES
BAKED TOMATOES AND BACON
PINEAPPLE SLAW WITH SOUR CREAM DRESSING   PRETZEL STICKS
BAKED BANANAS   COFFEE OR BEER
ASSORTED MINTS   SALTED NUTS

Stuffed Lobster Rolls

3 tablespoons butter
3 tablespoons flour
½ teaspoon salt
⅛ teaspoon pepper
¾ cup milk
⅓ cup grated Cheddar cheese

7-ounce can lobster meat, flaked
½ cup thinly-sliced celery
2 tablespoons finely-chopped
    green pepper
¼ cup sherry wine (optional)
6 large hard rolls

Melt butter in saucepan; add flour, salt, pepper and milk; cook until thickened, stirring constantly. Add cheese and stir until melted. Remove from heat and fold in lobster, celery, green pepper and sherry wine. Chill mixture for 2 hours. ½ hour before serving time, cut long thin slice from top of each roll and hollow out to form a shell. Fill shells with chilled mixture and replace thin slices on top of rolls. Wrap each roll in waxed paper or aluminum foil, and arrange on cooky sheet. When baked, remove paper and serve piping hot.

Baked Tomatoes and Bacon

2 tomatoes, sliced in thirds
¼ cup flour
1 egg, well beaten

3 drops Tabasco sauce
1 cup fine cracker crumbs
6 strips of bacon

Dip tomato slices in flour, then in mixture of egg and Tabasco sauce, and lastly in cracker crumbs. Place tomato slices in greased baking pan. Dip bacon slices first in egg mixture and then in cracker crumbs, and place on top of tomato slices.

Baked Bananas

3 bananas
1/4 cup lemon juice
1 egg, well beaten

1/4 cup tart jam
1/2 cup cake crumbs

Cut bananas in half, lengthwise; then crosswise. Dip each piece in lemon juice, then in beaten egg. Place in greased baking pan, cut-side down. Pour remaining lemon juice over banana slices and top each with jam. Sprinkle with cake crumbs.

Baking Directions

Place rolls on lower shelf in oven. Place tomatoes and bananas on shelf directly above. Set thermostat at hot, 425° F., and bake 25 minutes.

Nice Extra: Pineapple Slaw with Sour Cream Dressing

1 quart shredded cabbage
1 can crushed pineapple, drained
1 green pepper, chopped
1/4 cup vinegar

3/4 cup sour cream
2 tablespoons sugar
1/4 teaspoon salt
1 1/2 teaspoons prepared mustard

Combine cabbage, pineapple and green pepper in large salad bowl. Blend remaining ingredients together; pour over vegetables and toss gently.

Menu 73. Lobster Cutlets for Five
(30-MINUTE OVEN TIME)

RAW RELISH TRAY

LOBSTER CUTLETS   TARTARE SAUCE

POTATOES AU GRATIN   BAKED BRUSSELS SPROUTS

ASSORTED BREADS IN BASKET   BUTTER

COCONUT-RASPBERRY SQUARES   TEA

Lobster Cutlets

2 cups cooked lobster meat
¼ teaspoon salt
¼ teaspoon dry mustard
1 teaspoon lemon juice

1 cup condensed mushroom
    soup
1 cup fine bread crumbs
1 egg, beaten
1 tablespoon water

Combine lobster, salt, mustard, lemon juice and soup; shape into 5 cutlets about 1 inch thick. Dip each cutlet into bread crumbs, then egg beaten with water, and again in bread crumbs. Place in 9-inch-square greased pan.

Potatoes au Gratin

3 tablespoons butter
3 tablespoons flour
½ teaspoon salt
⅛ teaspoon pepper
¼ teaspoon dry mustard

2 cups milk
6 medium-sized boiled potatoes
1 cup grated American cheese
¼ cup bread crumbs

Melt butter in saucepan; add flour, salt, pepper and mustard. Slowly pour in milk and cook until mixture thickens, stirring constantly. Dice potatoes into ½-inch cubes; place them in greased 8-inch-square baking pan. Pour sauce over potatoes and sprinkle with mixture of cheese and crumbs.

Baked Brussels Sprouts

2½ cups Brussels sprouts
4 tablespoons butter
1 tablespoon onion juice

2 tablespoons lemon juice
½ teaspoon salt

Wash sprouts, cut in half and soak in cold, salted water for 15 minutes. Melt butter in saucepan; add onion juice, lemon juice, salt and blend. Drain sprouts and stir carefully into butter mixture. Cover tightly.

Coconut-Raspberry Squares

3 tablespoons raspberry jam
6 slices pound cake, ½ inch
   thick

1 can sweetened condensed
   milk
1½ cups shredded coconut

Spread raspberry jam on 3 slices of cake; top with the other 3 slices. Cut in half to form squares and dip in condensed milk; roll in coconut. Place in greased 7-by 9-inch baking pan.

Baking Directions

Place Brussels sprouts and coconut-raspberry squares on lower shelf in oven; place lobster and potatoes on shelf directly above. Set thermostat at hot, 400° F., and bake 30 minutes.

Added Attraction: Raw Relish Tray

Celery sticks
Carrot sticks or curls
Radishes

Olives
Pickles

Arrange on large, colorful chop plate.

Menu 74. Tuna Loaf for Six

(75-MINUTE OVEN TIME)

TUNA LOAF

STUFFED BAKED POTATOES   SPINACH WITH SIEVED EGG

RAISIN-NUT PUDDING WITH CARAMEL SAUCE   COFFEE

(DRIED FRUIT COMPOTE FOR TOMORROW, MENU 59)

Tuna Loaf

2½ cups flaked tuna	¾ cup cracker crumbs
½ teaspoon salt	2 tablespoons melted butter
¼ teaspoon paprika	1 cup tomato juice
⅛ teaspoon pepper	3 eggs, separated

Mix tuna, salt, paprika, pepper, cracker crumbs, butter and to-mato juice. Add beaten egg yolks and fold in stiffly-beaten egg whites. Pour into well-greased loaf pan.

Stuffed Baked Potatoes

6 medium-sized potatoes	1 teaspoon salt
2 tablespoons shortening	¼ teaspoon pepper
3 tablespoons butter	2 tablespoons hot milk

Wash potatoes. Dry, and rub with shortening. Prick with sharp fork and place in baking pan. After potatoes are baked, cut slice from top; scoop out potato, mash and season with butter, salt, pepper and hot milk. Refill shells. Place 5 inches from broiler for 5 minutes to reheat and brown.

Spinach

2 packages frozen spinach	¼ teaspoon salt
3 tablespoons butter	⅛ teaspoon pepper
¼ cup water	1 hard-cooked egg

Place spinach, butter and water in saucepan. Cover tightly. Before serving, drain, season with salt and pepper, and garnish with hard-cooked egg pressed through a sieve.

Raisin-Nut Pudding

½ cup shortening	2½ teaspoons baking powder
1 cup sugar	½ teaspoon salt
2 eggs	⅔ cup milk
1 teaspoon vanilla	¾ cup seedless raisins
2 cups sifted cake flour	½ cup chopped walnuts

Cream shortening and sugar until light and fluffy. Add eggs one at a time, beating thoroughly after each addition. Add vanilla. Sift together flour, baking powder and salt; add alternately with milk to egg mixture. Add raisins and walnuts to last ¼ cup of flour. Pour into greased and wax-paper-lined loaf pan. Bake.

CARAMEL SAUCE

¾ cup brown sugar	2 tablespoons butter
2 tablespoons flour	1 teaspoon vanilla
1 cup hot water	

Combine sugar and flour. Add hot water. Cook, stirring constantly until mixture boils. Continue cooking slowly for 5 minutes, stirring occasionally. Add butter and vanilla. Serve hot on raisin-nut pudding.

Baking Directions

In a cold oven place spinach and potatoes on lower shelf. On shelf directly above, place tuna loaf and raisin-nut pudding. Set oven control at moderate, 350° F., and turn on heat. Bake 75 minutes. Broil potatoes 5 minutes.

Menu 75. Tuna Economy Casserole for Four

(25-MINUTE OVEN TIME)

TUNA ECONOMY CASSEROLE

POTATO NESTS

DROPPED CHEESE BISCUITS   BUTTER

ITALIAN SALAD

SLICED FRESH PEACHES   RAISIN POUND CAKE *   TEA

*(Buy this.)

Tuna Economy Casserole

7-ounce can tuna, flaked
2 cups cooked elbow macaroni
1 can condensed mushroom
    soup

3 tablespoons milk
1 tablespoon parsley flakes
1 cup leftover vegetables
½ cup crushed potato chips

Combine flaked tuna, macaroni, soup, milk, parsley and vegetables. Pour into 1½-quart casserole; sprinkle with crushed potato chips.

Potato Nests

4 large hot cooked potatoes
3 tablespoons butter
2 tablespoons flour
1 tablespoon milk

3 tablespoons grated American
    cheese
½ teaspoon salt
¼ teaspoon pepper
1 cup stewed tomatoes

Mash potatoes with butter, flour, milk, cheese, salt and pepper. Blend well and shape into 4 large patties about 2 inches thick. Place in 8-inch greased baking pan; make a large hole in the center of each patty and fill with tomatoes.

Dropped Cheese Biscuits

2 cups sifted all-purpose flour
4 teaspoons baking powder
1 teaspoon salt
2 tablespoons shortening
½ cup grated American cheese
¾ cup milk

Sift together flour, baking powder and salt; cut in shortening and add grated cheese. Pour milk in all at once and blend with a fork. Roll dough into 1½-inch balls and place on cooky sheet.

Baking Directions

Place tuna casserole and potato nests on lower shelf in oven. Place biscuits on shelf directly above. Set thermostat at hot, 425° F., and bake 25 minutes.

Tempting Extra: Italian Salad

½ clove garlic, peeled
1 small head lettuce
2 firm tomatoes, cut in small pieces
4 radishes, sliced
2 tablespoons chopped green pepper
½ cucumber, peeled and sliced thin
¼ cup olive oil
½ teaspoon salt
½ teaspoon pepper
1 tablespoon wine vinegar

Rub large salad bowl with garlic. Shred lettuce into bowl, add tomatoes, radishes, green pepper and cucumber. Combine olive oil, salt, pepper and vinegar; pour over vegetables and toss gently.

Menu 76. Meat Balls for Six
(75-MINUTE OVEN TIME)

MEAT BALLS AND BROWN GRAVY   TOMATO CATSUP

LIMA BEANS   BAKED POTATOES

EGG BREAD   BUTTER

FRESH FRUIT BOWL   SUGARED CUPCAKES *   COFFEE

*(Buy these.)

Meat Balls

2 pounds ground beef
½ teaspoon prepared mustard
1 tablespoon Worcestershire
    sauce

¼ cup finely-chopped onion
⅛ teaspoon pepper
⅔ cup milk
¼ cup soft butter

Blend all ingredients. Divide into 6 portions and shape into ¾-inch-thick patties. Place in well-greased baking pan. Rub top of each patty with soft butter.

BROWN GRAVY

4 tablespoons butter
3 tablespoons browned flour
½ teaspoon salt
¼ teaspoon sugar

⅛ teaspoon pepper
1½ cups meat drippings and
    water

Melt butter; add flour, salt, sugar and pepper. Stir to smooth paste. Add the liquid, stirring until well blended. Cook until smooth and thickened.

Note: Flour is browned by stirring slowly in frying pan over low heat. Meat fat may be substituted for butter.

Lima Beans

2 packages frozen Lima beans   ¼ teaspoon salt
3 tablespoons butter   ⅛ teaspoon pepper
¼ cup water

Place Lima beans, butter and water in saucepan. Cover tightly. Before serving, season with salt and pepper.

Egg Bread

3 cups sifted southern corn   3 tablespoons sugar
   meal   2½ cups milk
3 teaspoons baking powder   ¼ cup melted butter
1½ teaspoons salt   3 eggs

Mix together corn meal, baking powder, salt and sugar. Add milk slowly, beating until free of lumps. Add butter and beaten eggs. Pour into greased 7-by 11-inch baking pan.

Baked Potatoes

6 potatoes   2 tablespoons shortening

Wash potatoes. Dry thoroughly and prick with sharp fork. Rub with shortening; place in 7-by 11-inch baking pan.

Baking Directions

In a cold oven place meat balls and Lima beans on lower shelf. On shelf directly above, place egg bread and potatoes. Set oven control at moderate, 350° F., and turn oven on. Bake 75 minutes.

Menu 77. Baked Ham for Six

(75-MINUTE OVEN TIME)

CHICKEN BROTH WITH RICE   SALTINES
BAKED HAM WITH JELLY SAUCE
CHEESE-AND-POTATO SCALLOP   HOT CROSS BUNS *
WATER-CRESS AND GRAPEFRUIT SALAD
APPLE CANDY PUDDING WITH CREAM   COFFEE

*(Buy these.)

Baked Ham with Jelly Sauce

4-pound precooked ham	1 quart sweet cider
1 cup brown sugar	½ cup currant jelly
¼ teaspoon cinnamon	¼ cup prepared mustard
Whole cloves	

Rub ham with brown sugar mixed with cinnamon. Stick cloves in ham. Place in roasting pan and cover with cider. Baste frequently. Serve with jelly sauce made by mixing currant jelly and prepared mustard. Beat with egg beater until creamy.

Cheese-and-Potato Scallop

3 cups raw potatoes, sliced	¾ cup evaporated milk
1½ cups soft bread crumbs	¾ cup water
1 cup grated Cheddar cheese	½ teaspoon salt
2 onions, sliced thin	¼ teaspoon pepper
2 tablespoons butter	⅛ teaspoon cayenne pepper

Soak potatoes in cold water for 1 hour. Drain. Sprinkle bottom of greased casserole with crumbs. Fill casserole with alternate layers of potatoes, cheese, onions and crumbs. Melt butter in diluted milk which has been warmed slightly. Add salt, pepper and cayenne pepper. Pour over potatoes.

Apple Candy Pudding

8 medium-sized tart apples	¾ cup all-purpose flour
¾ cup white sugar	1 cup brown sugar
¼ teaspoon nutmeg	½ cup butter
⅓ cup red cinnamon candies	1 cup cream

Place in buttered baking dish a layer of sliced apples. Sprinkle with sugar mixed with nutmeg and candies. Alternate apples and sugar mixture. Mix flour and brown sugar. Cut in butter. Spread over top of mixture and bake. Serve warm or cold with cream.

Baking Directions

In a cold oven place ham and apple pudding on lower shelf. On shelf directly above, place cheese-and-potato scallop. Set thermostat at moderate, 350° F. Turn on heat and bake 75 minutes. Heat buns during last 10 minutes.

Nice Extra: Water-Cress and Grapefruit Salad

1 bunch water-cress	½ cup French dressing
18 sections of grapefruit	

Pick over water-cress, wash and chill. Arrange grapefruit sections on bed of water-cress. Pour over French dressing.

Menu 78. Ham-Stuffed Peppers for Six
(75-MINUTE OVEN TIME)

HAM-STUFFED GREEN PEPPERS

HARVARD BEETS   SQUASH SOUFFLÉ   BREAD STICKS *   BUTTER

ITALIAN SALAD (MENU 75)

GINGERCAKE WITH WHIPPED CREAM   COFFEE

*(Buy these.)

Ham-Stuffed Green Peppers

6 green peppers
1½ cups ground ham
4 slices crisp cooked bacon,
    chopped
2 cups boiled rice

2 tablespoons melted butter
2 tablespoons chopped onion
⅛ teaspoon pepper
1 cup diced tomatoes
½ cup water

Cut stem end from peppers. Remove seeds and white sections. Wash and drain. Mix ham, bacon, rice, butter, onion, pepper and tomatoes. Pile into peppers. Place in greased 9-inch pan; add ½ cup of water and bake.

Harvard Beets

12 medium-sized beets
¾ cup water
2 tablespoons butter
¼ teaspoon salt

2 tablespoons flour
⅓ cup vinegar
½ cup sugar
⅓ cup water from beets

Wash beets. Pare and slice, and place in 1-quart pan; add water. Cover tightly and bake. Before serving, drain off beet juice, saving ⅓ cup. Melt butter; add salt and flour. Stir until smooth. Add vinegar, sugar and beet juice. Cook until thick and clear. Add cooked beets and toss until coated.

Squash Soufflé

¼ cup butter	1 teaspoon salt
2½ tablespoons flour	⅛ teaspoon pepper
1 cup milk	2 eggs, separated
2 cups cooked mashed squash	¾ cup cracker crumbs
2 teaspoons onion juice	

Melt butter; add flour and stir until smooth. Add milk slowly and cook until thick and smooth, stirring constantly. Drain squash thoroughly before measuring. Squash must be dry. Add onion, salt, pepper, egg yolks and cracker crumbs. Stir until well blended. Add white sauce and mix well. Beat egg whites stiff but not dry. Fold into squash. Pour into greased 1½-quart casserole.

Gingercake

½ cup shortening	2 teaspoons ginger
½ cup sugar	¼ teaspoon salt
2 eggs	¾ teaspoon baking soda
1 cup dark molasses	1 teaspoon baking powder
3 cups sifted flour	1 cup hot water
1 teaspoon cloves	1 pint heavy cream, whipped
1 teaspoon cinnamon	

Cream shortening and sugar. Add eggs and beat until creamy. Add molasses; beat until smooth. Sift flour, cloves, cinnamon, ginger, salt, soda and baking powder together. Add to molasses mixture. Stir in hot water last. Pour into greased loaf pan.

Baking Directions

In cold oven place peppers and beets on lower shelf. On shelf directly above, place squash and gingercake. Set thermostat at moderate, 350° F., and turn oven on. Bake 75 minutes.

Menu 79. Spinach-Ham Timbales for Six

(50-MINUTE OVEN TIME)

SPINACH-HAM TIMBALES   PICKLE RELISH

QUICK SCALLOPED POTATOES

GOLDEN DINNER SALAD   CLOVERLEAF ROLLS *   BUTTER

QUICK COFFEECAKE   COFFEE

*(Buy these.)

Spinach-Ham Timbales

¼ cup chopped onion

¼ cup chopped green pepper

2 tablespoons butter

1 egg, beaten

1 pound ground smoked ham

½ cup soft bread crumbs

¼ teaspoon salt

⅛ teaspoon pepper

1 cup cooked spinach

Brown onion and green pepper in butter. Blend egg, ground ham, bread crumbs, salt and pepper; combine with browned ingredients. Divide mixture in half and pack half in equal layers in 6 greased custard cups. Add a layer of spinach and top with a third layer of the remaining ham mixture. Set filled custard cups in pan of water and bake.

Quick Scalloped Potatoes

6 baking potatoes

1 quart water

1 teaspoon salt

2 tablespoons butter

2 tablespoons flour

1 cup milk

¼ teaspoon salt

Dash of pepper

2 tablespoons grated American cheese

Wash and pare potatoes and slice thin. Cook in 1 quart of water with 1 teaspoon salt until almost tender. Drain well and place in greased 2½-quart casserole. Melt butter in a saucepan, stir in flour and slowly add milk. Cook until smooth. As mixture thickens, add ¼ teaspoon salt, pepper and grated cheese, stirring constantly. Pour sauce over potatoes.

Quick Coffeecake

1 egg, beaten
¾ cup milk
⅓ cup shortening, melted
1 tablespoon grated orange rind
2 cups all-purpose flour
2 teaspoons baking powder
1 teaspoon salt
½ teaspoon nutmeg

¼ cup sugar
⅓ cup chopped nuts
⅓ cup fine bread crumbs
3 tablespoons flour
1½ teaspoons cinnamon
½ cup confectioners sugar
3 tablespoons melted butter

Combine the egg, milk, shortening and orange rind. Sift together the 2 cups of flour, baking powder, salt, nutmeg and ¼ cup of sugar, and add to first mixture. Stir in chopped nuts and turn into greased 9-inch baking pan. Combine bread crumbs, 3 tablespoons flour, cinnamon and confectioners sugar. Blend well and toss with melted butter to form coarse crumbs. Place crumbs on cake batter. Sprinkle with additional confectioners sugar before serving, if desired.

Baking Directions

Place spinach-ham timbales on lower shelf in oven; on shelf directly above place coffeecake and scalloped potatoes. Set thermostat at moderate, 350° F., and bake 40 minutes. Remove spinach-ham timbales and scalloped potatoes, and continue baking coffee cake and heat rolls for 10 minutes longer, or 50 minutes total oven time.

Colorful Extra: Golden Dinner Salad

1 package lemon-flavored
    gelatin
2 cups water
1½ teaspoons vinegar
¼ teaspoon salt

¾ cup grapefruit sections
¾ cup grated raw carrot
Lettuce leaves
Mayonnaise

Dissolve gelatin in water according to directions on package; add vinegar and salt, and chill until slightly thickened. Fold in grapefruit sections and grated carrots; turn into 6 individual molds. Chill until firm. Unmold on lettuce leaves and top each with mayonnaise.

Menu 80. Pork Chop Specialty Luncheon for Four
(50-MINUTE OVEN TIME)

BAKED GRAPEFRUIT WITH WINE
PORK CHOP SPECIALTY   BAKED APPLESAUCE
HOT CRUSTY ROLLS *   BUTTER   SWEET MIXED PICKLES
BROWNIES WITH VANILLA ICE CREAM   COFFEE

*(Buy these.)

Baked Grapefruit with Wine

2 grapefruit, cut in half   4 tablespoons melted butter
4 tablespoons brown sugar   4 tablespoons port wine

Section grapefruit halves with sharp knife. Sprinkle each half with brown sugar, melted butter and port wine and set in 9- by 12-inch pan.

Pork Chop Specialty

4 pork chops, ¾ inch thick   ½ cup canned tomatoes
1 cup cooked rice   4 green pepper rings
1 Bermuda onion, cut in 4 slices

Brown chops on both sides in frying pan and place them in a large, greased 9-inch-square pan. Top each chop with ¼ cup rice, 1 slice onion, 2 tablespoons tomatoes and a pepper ring.

Baked Applesauce

1 quart cold water	½ teaspoon cinnamon
1 teaspoon salt	2 teaspoons butter
3 cups thinly-sliced apples	2 tablespoons water
½ cup sugar	

Combine cold water, salt and sliced apples; blend together sugar and cinnamon. Drain apples and toss with sugar mixture. Place butter and 2 tablespoons water in 2-quart casserole dish, add sugared apples and cover tightly.

Brownies

½ cup shortening	¾ cup all-purpose flour
2 one-ounce squares unsweet-	½ teaspoon baking powder
ened chocolate	½ teaspoon salt
2 eggs, well beaten	1 teaspoon vanilla
1 cup sugar	1 cup chopped walnuts

Melt shortening and chocolate over hot water and set aside to cool. Combine beaten eggs, sugar and cooled chocolate mixture. Sift together flour, baking powder and salt, and add to first mixture with vanilla. Beat thoroughly and fold in chopped walnuts. Pour batter into 8-inch-square, greased and waxed-paper-lined baking pan. Cool before cutting, and top with ice cream when served.

Baking Directions

Place pork chops and applesauce on lower shelf in oven; place brownies on shelf directly above. Turn heat on and set thermostat at moderate, 350° F. At the end of 35 minutes baking time remove applesauce and add grapefruit. Add rolls and continue baking 15 minutes longer. Total baking time 50 minutes.

Menu 81. Veal Birds for Six

(75-MINUTE OVEN TIME)

CREAM OF TOMATO SOUP   OYSTER CRACKERS

VEAL BIRDS

FRESH ASPARAGUS   POTATOES IN CASSEROLE

CRACKED-WHEAT BREAD *   BUTTER

FIG UPSIDE-DOWN CAKE   NUTMEG-CREAM   COFFEE

*(Buy this.)

Veal Birds

2 cups stale bread cubes
3 tablespoons melted butter
½ teaspoon salt
⅛ teaspoon pepper
¼ cup finely-chopped onion
2 tablespoons chopped parsley
¼ cup orange juice

6 thin slices veal, cut 4 by 5
    inches
⅓ cup flour
½ teaspoon salt
⅛ teaspoon pepper
¼ cup fat

Mix together bread, butter, salt, pepper, onion, parsley and orange juice. Pile dressing on veal slices. Roll veal; fasten with skewers or tie with string. Blend flour, salt and pepper. Flour veal rolls and brown quickly in hot fat. Place on rack in casserole. Cover tightly.

Fresh Asparagus

1 bunch fresh asparagus
½ teaspoon salt
1 cup water

¼ cup melted butter
⅛ teaspoon pepper

Cut off tough stalks. Trim all leaves from stem to tip. Wash. Place in 2-quart saucepan; add salt and water. Cover tightly. Just before serving, drain and add butter and pepper.

Potatoes in Casserole

8 potatoes   ¼ cup butter
½ teaspoon salt   2 tablespoons water
⅛ teaspoon pepper

Pare and slice potatoes. Place in greased 2½-quart casserole.
Sprinkle with salt and pepper. Dot with butter; add water and
cover tightly.

Fig Upside-Down Cake

⅓ cup butter   ⅓ cup fig juice
1 cup brown sugar   1 cup sifted cake flour
6 canned figs   1½ teaspoons baking powder
6 maraschino cherries   ¼ teaspoon salt
3 eggs, separated   ½ teaspoon vanilla
1 cup sugar

Melt butter; add sugar and blend. Pack on bottom of greased
loaf pan. Remove stems from figs, cut in half and arrange with
cherries on top of sugar mixture. Beat egg yolks until thick; add
sugar and continue beating. Add fig juice. Sift flour, baking
powder and salt together. Fold into egg-yolk mixture. Beat egg
whites and vanilla stiff but not dry. Fold into cake mixture.
Pour over figs and bake.

NUTMEG-CREAM

2 tablespoons sugar   ½ teaspoon vanilla
¼ teaspoon nutmeg   ½ pint light cream

Mix sugar and nutmeg. Add vanilla and cream. Stir until sugar is
dissolved.

Baking Directions

Into cold oven place veal and asparagus on lower shelf in oven.
On shelf directly above, place potatoes and fig cake. Set thermostat at moderate, 350° F., and turn oven on. Bake 75 minutes.

Menu 82. Veal de Luxe for Six
(2-HOUR OVEN TIME)

SHERRIED LEG OF VEAL   CRISP CELERY AND DILL PICKLES

SWEET POTATOES WITH PINEAPPLE

CAULIFLOWER IN MUSHROOM SAUCE

SALT STICKS *   BUTTER

CRANBERRY-PECAN SALAD WITH CREAM-CHEESE DRESSING (MENU 52)

CALIFORNIA FRUIT CUP   LEMON COOKIES *   COFFEE

*(Buy these.)

Sherried Leg of Veal

4½-pound leg of veal
1 tablespoon prepared mustard
1 teaspoon sage
1 tablespoon brown sugar
1 teaspoon salt

⅛ teaspoon pepper
2 tablespoons lemon juice
6 slices bacon
¾ cup hot water
½ cup sherry

Wipe meat and place on rack in roasting pan. Mix together mustard, sage, sugar, salt, pepper and lemon juice. Spread over veal. Arrange bacon over meat and add hot water and sherry. Cover.

Sweet Potatoes with Pineapple

6 medium-sized sweet potatoes
½ teaspoon salt
⅛ teaspoon pepper
4 pineapple slices

¾ cup dark brown sugar
⅛ teaspoon ginger
2 tablespoons butter
½ cup pineapple juice

Wash, peel and slice potatoes lengthwise into ½-inch slices. Place in greased 9 by 11 inch pan. Season with salt and pepper.

Cut pineapple slices into thirds and arrange over potatoes. Blend together sugar and ginger and cover potatoes with mixture. Dot with butter; add pineapple juice. Cover tightly. Use aluminum foil or parchment paper to make a cover.

Cauliflower in Mushroom Sauce

1 large cauliflower
1 can condensed mushroom
   soup

½ cup milk
1 teaspoon salt
⅛ teaspoon pepper

Wash cauliflower. Separate into flowerets; cut stems almost to flower. Into greased 2-quart casserole pour mushroom soup mixed with milk, salt and pepper. Put in cauliflower. Cover tightly.

Baking Directions

In a cold oven place veal on lower shelf; on shelf directly above, place potatoes. Set thermostat at moderate, 350° F. Turn on heat. At the end of 1¼ hours of baking time, remove cover from veal and baste meat. Remove cover from potatoes. Place cauliflower on shelf with veal. Bake 45 minutes longer with cover off veal and potatoes. Total oven time 2 hours.

Good Ending: California Fruit Cup

1 grapefruit
3 oranges
½ cup confectioners sugar

3 cups lemon sherbet
1½ cups undiluted grape juice

Peel and section both fruits, removing all membrane. Roll in confectioners sugar. Chill. Arrange over lemon sherbet. Add grape juice and serve at once.

Menu 83. Oven-Braised Veal for Four
(60-MINUTE OVEN TIME)

OVEN-BRAISED VEAL

SPANISH GREEN BEANS   SWEET POTATOES AND APPLES

RAW RELISH TRAY (MENU 31)   GERMAN PUMPERNICKEL *

BUTTER

BAKED FRUIT PUDDING   TEA

*(Buy this.)

Oven-Braised Veal

¼ cup flour
⅓ teaspoon salt
⅛ teaspoon pepper
4 veal chops

2 tablespoons shortening,
  melted
1¼ cups sour cream

Blend flour, salt and pepper. Dip chops in seasoned flour and brown on both sides in melted shortening. Place browned cutlets in greased 2½-quart casserole, pour over the sour cream and cover tightly.

Spanish Green Beans

⅔ cup diced bacon
½ cup chopped onion
2 tablespoons flour
1 bay leaf
½ teaspoon salt
¼ teaspoon pepper

¼ teaspoon paprika
2 cups cooked tomatoes
2 cups cooked green beans
1 cup coarse cracker crumbs
2 tablespoons butter, melted

Brown bacon and onion in large saucepan; add flour, bay leaf, salt, pepper, paprika, tomatoes and green beans. Blend ingredients thoroughly and pour into greased 1-quart casserole. Combine cracker crumbs and melted butter and sprinkle over green bean mixture.

Sweet Potatoes and Apples

3½ cups (No. 2½ can) sweet potatoes
2 tablespoons butter
1 teaspoon salt

⅛ teaspoon pepper
2 tablespoons cream
2 apples
8 marshmallows

Heat sweet potatoes and mash with butter, salt, pepper and cream. Spread potato mixture in 8-inch-square baking pan. Wash and core apples; cut in half but do not remove skins. Place apple halves on mashed potatoes and garnish with marshmallows.

Baked Fruit Pudding

3 cups soft bread crumbs
¼ cup melted butter
1 cup brown sugar
½ teaspoon cinnamon
¼ teaspoon nutmeg
2 bananas, sliced

2 cups rhubarb, cut in 1-inch pieces
1 cup applesauce
3 tablespoons light corn sirup
1 tablespoon lemon juice

Brown bread crumbs in melted butter. Combine sugar, cinnamon and nutmeg. In large, greased loaf pan place alternate layers of bread crumbs, sugar mixture, rhubarb, bananas and applesauce, starting and ending with bread crumbs. Top with a mixture of corn sirup and lemon juice.

Baking Directions

Place veal and green beans on lower shelf and sweet potatoes and fruit pudding on shelf directly above. Set thermostat at moderate, 375° F., and bake 60 minutes.

Menu 84. Vegetable Nut Loaf Dinner for Six

(50-MINUTE OVEN TIME)

VEGETABLE NUT LOAF   TOMATO SAUCE

BAKED STUFFED TURNIP

DINNER SALAD   BUTTERGEM ROLLS *

MINCEMEAT BROWNIES   BUTTER PECAN ICE CREAM   COFFEE

(CUPCAKES FOR TOMORROW, MENU 13)

*(Buy these.)

Vegetable Nut Loaf

2 eggs
¼ cup catsup
1 cup cooked rice
¼ cup fine bread crumbs

2 cups mixed canned or leftover
vegetables
½ cup finely-chopped nuts

Beat eggs and add remaining ingredients in order listed. Pack gently into greased loaf pan. Serve with tomato sauce.

TOMATO SAUCE

¼ cup butter
¼ cup flour
2½ cups (No. 2 can) tomatoes
1 teaspoon sugar

¾ teaspoon salt
1½ teaspoons grated onion
½ teaspoon Worcestershire
sauce

Melt butter, add flour and blend smooth. Add remaining ingredients and cook until thick and smooth. Stir frequently.

Baked Stuffed Turnip

1 large yellow turnip
1 quart boiling water
1 tablespoon salt
1 tablespoon sugar
2 tablespoons butter
¼ cup milk

¼ cup grated American cheese
1 cup soft bread crumbs
1 tablespoon chopped parsley
½ teaspoon salt
⅛ teaspoon pepper

Wash turnip and cut into quarters. Cook turnip in boiling water with 1 tablespoon salt and 1 tablespoon sugar. When tender, drain and remove pulp, leaving a 1-inch shell. Mash pulp with remaining ingredients in order given, fill the shells with this mixture and place in greased 8- by 10-inch pan.

Mincemeat Brownies

¼ cup butter
1 cup dark brown sugar
1 egg
½ teaspoon vanilla

½ cup mincemeat
1 cup flour
1¼ teaspoons baking powder
¼ teaspoon salt

Melt butter; add brown sugar and blend. Add unbeaten egg and beat until blended. Add vanilla and mincemeat, stirring until well mixed. Sift together flour, baking powder and salt. Add to mincemeat and mix together. Spread batter in greased 8-inch-square baking pan.

Baking Directions

Place vegetable loaf and turnip on lower shelf in oven; on shelf directly above, place cupcakes and brownies. Set thermostat at moderate, 375° F., and bake 50 minutes.

Tasty Extra: Dinner Salad

2 oranges, peeled and sliced
1 Spanish onion, sliced
1½ cups fresh cranberries, sliced

¼ cup French dressing
½ head lettuce

Marinate sliced oranges, onion and cranberries in French dressing for 30 minutes. Tear lettuce leaves into medium-sized pieces in salad bowl, add marinated fruit and blend thoroughly.

III

UNDER THE BROILER

Menu 85. Deviled Clams for Four
(14-MINUTE BROILING TIME)

DEVILED CLAMS   SWEET MUSTARD PICKLES

FRENCH FRIED POTATOES   LEMON CARROTS

KOMMISBROT *   BUTTER

COCONUT STRIPS   STRAWBERRY ICE CREAM   COFFEE

*(Buy this.)

Deviled Clams

2 No. 1 cans minced clams
2 tablespoons butter
3 tablespoons flour
¾ cup milk
1 egg yolk
1 tablespoon chopped parsley

1 tablespoon finely-chopped onion
⅛ teaspoon pepper
2 tablespoons grated Parmesan cheese
1 cup bread crumbs
2 tablespoons melted butter

Drain clams. Melt butter; add flour and stir until smooth. Add milk and cook, stirring constantly, until thickened. Beat egg yolk. Add some of the hot sauce to yolk. Add to remaining sauce and cook 1 minute, stirring constantly. Add parsley, onion, pepper and drained clams. Pile into greased clam shells. Sprinkle with cheese. Blend crumbs and melted butter. Sprinkle over cheese.

French Fried Potatoes

2 packages frozen French fried potatoes

Coconut Strips

2 slices day-old bread
¼ teaspoon grated lemon rind
1 teaspoon lemon juice

⅓ cup sweetened condensed
   milk
⅓ cup moist shredded coconut

Remove crusts from bread. Cut each slice into 4 strips. Add lemon rind and juice to condensed milk. Pour into pie plate. Roll bread strips in milk mixture and then in coconut.

Broiling Directions

Separate frozen potatoes and place in broiler pan. Cover with rack. Place coconut strips on rack and place pan so that heat source is 4 inches from top of coconut. Broil 2 minutes. Turn strips and broil 2 minutes longer. Remove coconut strips. Remove rack and stir potatoes. Replace rack. Place clam shells on rack. Broil ten minutes. Total broiling time 14 minutes.

Note: If large clam shells are not available spread clam mixture in shallow baking pan, and serve on buttered toast rounds.

Lemon Carrots

2½ cups (No. 2 can) diced
   carrots
2 tablespoons butter
1 tablespoon sugar

½ teaspoon paprika
1 tablespoon lemon juice
⅛ teaspoon pepper
1 tablespoon chopped parsley

Drain carrots. Melt butter. Add sugar, paprika, lemon juice and pepper. Mix well. Add carrots and heat, stirring occasionally. Add parsley just before serving.

Menu 86. Halibut Steak for Four

(10-MINUTE BROILING TIME)

HALIBUT STEAK WITH OYSTER SAUCE   SWEET GHERKINS

POTATOES WITH CHEESE   PEAS AND ONIONS

FRENCH BREAD *   BUTTER

BING CHERRY COMPOTE   WALNUT COOKIES *   COFFEE

*(Buy these.)

Halibut Steak

1½ pounds halibut steak
2 tablespoons lemon juice
½ teaspoon salt

⅛ teaspoon pepper
2 tablespoons butter

Wipe halibut with damp cloth. Rub lemon juice over fish. Sprinkle with salt and pepper. Dot one side with 1 tablespoon butter. Use remaining butter for other side after turning fish.

OYSTER SAUCE

3 tablespoons butter
3 tablespoons flour
¼ teaspoon salt
⅛ teaspoon pepper
1 cup hot milk

1 dozen oysters, chopped, with liquor
1 teaspoon lemon juice
1 tablespoon chopped parsley

Melt butter; add flour, salt and pepper. Stir until smooth. Slowly add milk, stirring constantly until smooth and thickened. Add oysters and oyster liquor. Heat through but do not boil. Add lemon juice and parsley. Serve with broiled fish.

Potatoes with Cheese

3 large potatoes
1 quart boiling water
1 teaspoon salt

½ cup grated Cheddar cheese
⅛ teaspoon pepper

Wash potatoes. Pare and cut lengthwise into 4 slices each. Place in boiling salted water. Parboil until almost done. Drain and cover each slice of potato with cheese. Sprinkle slices with pepper.

Peas and Onions

2 medium-sized onions
2½ cups (No. 2 can) peas
¼ teaspoon salt

⅛ teaspoon pepper
1 tablespoon butter

Peel and thinly slice onions. Into saucepan drain juice from peas. Place onions in drained liquor and parboil 10 minutes. Drain onions; add to peas. Sprinkle with salt and pepper and dot with butter.

Broiling Directions

Grease broiler pan. Arrange potato slices in one end of pan. Place peas and onions at opposite end. Cover with broiler rack. Grease rack. Place halibut steaks on rack, buttered-side up. Place broiler pan so that top of fish is 2½ inches from source of heat. Broil 5 minutes. Turn fish carefully. Dot with remaining butter and broil 5 minutes longer. Total broiling time 10 minutes.

Bing Cherry Compote

2½ cups (No. 2 can) Bing
   cherries

4 canned pear halves
2 oranges, sectioned

Combine fruits and chill.

Menu 87. Broiled Mackerel for Six
(16-MINUTE BROILING TIME)

CELERY   OLIVES

BROILED MACKEREL WITH MUSTARD PARSLEY SAUCE

POTATO PUFFS   BUTTERED BROCCOLI

HOT CRUSTY ROLLS *   BUTTER

SLICED BANANAS AND CREAM   SUGAR-FILLED WAFERS *   COFFEE

*(Buy these.)

Mackerel

3-pound mackerel   1 teaspoon salt
1 tablespoon salad oil   ¼ teaspoon pepper

Split and bone mackerel. Mix oil, salt and pepper and brush over cut surface of fish.

MUSTARD PARSLEY SAUCE

2 tablespoons butter
1 teaspoon prepared mustard
1 teaspoon flour
2 tablespoons lemon juice
2 tablespoons chopped parsley

Cream butter and mustard together. Add flour and blend. Stir in lemon juice and parsley. Spread over broiled fish for last minute of broiling.

Potato Puffs

3 packages frozen potato puffs

Place potato puffs in greased broiler pan.

Broiling Directions

Cover potato puffs with sheet of aluminum foil to prevent fish juices from flavoring them. Cover with greased broiler rack. Lay fish, skin-side down, on rack. Have surface of fish 4 inches from heat source. Broil 15 minutes. Spread with mustard parsley sauce and broil 1 minute longer. Total broiling time 16 minutes. Heat rolls below broiler pan.

190

Menu 88. Broiled Smelts for Four

(8-MINUTE BROILING TIME)

BROILED SMELTS WITH LEMON WEDGES

RICE-STUFFED PEPPERSBUTTERED MIXED VEGETABLES

BRAN MUFFINS * BUTTER

FROZEN FRUIT SALAD CHEESE CRACKERS COFFEE

*(Buy these.)

Broiled Smelts

8 large smelts
3 tablespoons butter, melted
1 tablespoon lemon juice
1 teaspoon onion juice

2 teaspoons salt
½ teaspoon pepper
¼ cup flour
1 lemon, cut in quarters

Wash smelts. Remove heads and split so they will lie flat. Blend butter, lemon and onion juice, salt and pepper. Dip fish first in flour and then in seasoned butter; then again in flour. Serve with lemon wedges.

Rice-Stuffed Peppers

2 large green peppers
1 quart boiling water
¼ teaspoon baking soda
1 tablespoon salt

1 can Spanish rice
2 tablespoons grated Cheddar
    cheese

Cut peppers in half lengthwise. Remove seeds and membrane. Place in water to which soda and salt have been added. Simmer until tender. Drain. Fill with Spanish rice; top with grated cheese.

Mixed Vegetables

1 can mixed vegetables	¼ teaspoon salt
2 tablespoons butter	⅛ teaspoon pepper

Drain vegetables. Mix with butter, salt and pepper. Place in broiler pan.

Broiling Directions

Place rack over vegetables. Arrange floured smelts in center of broiler pan and stuffed peppers at the corners. Place broiler pan so that surface of peppers is 3 inches from source of heat. Broil 8 minutes.

Frozen Fruit Salad

6 ounces (2 packages) cream cheese	4 peach halves, cubed
¼ cup sugar	½ cup maraschino cherries, drained
1 cup mayonnaise	¾ cup chopped pecans
4 slices pineapple, diced	1 cup heavy cream, whipped

Cream the cheese, add sugar, mayonnaise, pineapple, peaches, cherries cut in half, and pecans. Fold in whipped cream. Pour into freezer tray and freeze at coldest temperature for 4 hours. When serving, pass your favorite dressing if desired.

Menu 89. Broiled Chicken for Four
(25-MINUTE BROILING TIME)

BROILED CHICKEN   RIPE OLIVES   SWEET GHERKINS

CREAMED POTATOES   CORN ON THE COB

SALT STICKS *   BUTTER

ITALIAN SALAD (MENU 75)

GINGER PARFAIT   SPONGECAKE *   COFFEE

*(Buy these.)

Broiled Chicken

2 chicken breasts
2 chicken legs
½ teaspoon salt

⅛ teaspoon pepper
½ teaspoon paprika
¼ cup melted butter

Wipe chicken with damp cloth. Season with salt, pepper and paprika. Brush with melted butter.

Creamed Potatoes

5 boiled potatoes
3 tablespoons butter
3 tablespoons flour
2 teaspoons prepared mustard

½ teaspoon salt
⅛ teaspoon pepper
1½ cups milk
½ cup grated Cheddar cheese

Peel and dice cooked potatoes. Melt butter; add flour. Stir until smooth. Add mustard, salt and pepper, and blend. Add milk slowly. Cook until smooth and thickened. Add potatoes to sauce. Turn into greased broiler pan. Top with cheese.

Corn on the Cob

4 ears of corn	¼ teaspoon salt
2 tablespoons melted butter	⅛ teaspoon pepper

Remove husks and silk from corn. Brush with melted butter. Season with salt and pepper.

Broiling Directions

Place rack over potatoes in broiler pan. Place chicken, bone side up, on rack. Arrange corn at sides. Broil 8 minutes. Turn corn and chicken and brush both with butter. Broil 8 minutes. Turn again and brush with butter, and broil 9 minutes longer. Total broiling time 25 minutes.

Ginger Parfait

1 cup sugar	2 cups heavy cream, whipped
¼ cup water	½ cup preserved ginger,
3 egg whites	chopped fine
¼ cup ginger sirup	½ cup chopped pecans
1 tablespoon vanilla	¼ cup red raspberry jam

Boil sugar and water together until sirup reaches 238° F., or until it threads when dropped from spoon. Beat egg whites stiff but not dry. Slowly add hot sirup, beating constantly. Beat until cold. Add ginger sirup and vanilla. Fold in whipped cream, chopped ginger and nut meats. Pour into freezer ice tray and freeze. Serve in parfait glasses with raspberry jam.

Menu 90. Chicken Livers Norman for Four

(18-MINUTE BROILING TIME)

CHICKEN LIVERS EN BROCHETTE   SAUERKRAUT RELISH

SPANISH RICE

HARD ROLLS *   BUTTER

RASPBERRY SHEBRET   ALMOND COOKIES *   COFFEE

* (Buy these.)

Chicken Livers en Brochette

¼ cup wine vinegar
¼ cup dry red wine
1 medium-sized onion, sliced
1 clove garlic, crushed
1 bay leaf
2 tablespoons olive oil
12 chicken livers

8 large fresh mushrooms
1 quart boiling water
8 small white onions
2 firm ripe tomatoes
¼ cup butter
1 teaspoon Worcestershire
sauce

Mix together wine vinegar, red wine, sliced onion, garlic, bay leaf and olive oil. Pour over chicken livers; mix and refrigerate overnight. Wash mushrooms. Place in boiling water 5 minutes. Drain. Cook onions until almost tender. Cut tomatoes in quarters. Use 4 ten-inch skewers. Place on each skewer 3 pieces of livers, 2 mushrooms, 2 onions, and 2 pieces of tomato. Start and end with liver. Brush well with butter mixed with Worcester-shire sauce.

Spanish Rice

4 cups canned Spanish rice
1 tablespoon butter

¼ cup crushed corn flakes

Broiling Directions

Grease broiler. Spread Spanish rice 1 inch thick in center. Sprin-kle with buttered corn flakes. Place broiler rack over rice. Place brochettes on rack. Set rack so that surface of meat is 4 inches from heat source. Broil 18 minutes, turning frequently and bast-ing with the butter and Worcestershire sauce. Heat rolls below broiler pan.

Sauerkraut Relish

1 No. 2 can sauerkraut
1 cup chili sauce
⅓ cup brown sugar
1 teaspoon paprika
1/16 teaspoon red pepper

3 tablespoons lemon juice
1 green pepper, chopped fine
1 small onion, chopped fine
3 stalks celery, chopped fine

Mix all ingredients together thoroughly. Place in refrigerator. Serve very cold.

Menu 91. Hamburger Cutlets for Four
(7-MINUTE BROILING TIME)

CELERY   RADISHES

HAMBURGER CUTLETS   LEMON-PARSLEY SAUCE

BROWNED POTATOES   CRUSTY CARROTS

BUTTERGEM ROLLS *   BUTTER

MACAROONS *   CHOCOLATE MINT ICE CREAM   COFFEE

* (Buy these.)

Hamburger Cutlets

1 pound ground beef
½ teaspoon salt
1 teaspoon Worcestershire
    sauce

¼ teaspoon pepper
1 small onion, chopped fine
1 teaspoon horse-radish
1 tablespoon chili sauce

Combine all ingredients and mix well. Shape into 4 inch-thick patties and then into cutlet shape.

LEMON-PARSLEY SAUCE

1½ tablespoons butter
2 teaspoons lemon juice

2 tablespoons chopped parsley
1 drop Tabasco sauce

Cream butter; add lemon juice, parsley and Tabasco sauce and blend. Serve on top of hamburger cutlets.

Browned Potatoes

4 cooked potatoes
2 tablespoons melted butter
½ teaspoon onion juice

¼ teaspoon salt
⅛ teaspoon pepper

Peel and cut potatoes into small cubes. Combine butter, onion juice, salt and pepper. Toss cubed potatoes in mixture until all are coated.

Crusty Carrots

8 small cooked whole carrots
2 tablespoons melted butter

½ cup crushed corn flakes
1 tablespoon sugar

Dip carrots in melted butter. Mix corn flakes and sugar. Roll carrots in corn flakes.

Broiling Directions

Grease broiler pan. Spread potatoes at one end and carrots at the other. Place rack over vegetables. Arrange cutlets on rack. Place broiler pan so that surface of meat is 2 inches from source of heat. Broil 4 minutes. Turn meat and broil 3 minutes longer. Total broiling time 7 minutes. Warm rolls below broiler pan.

Menu 92. Hawaiian Short Ribs for Four

(20-MINUTE BROILING TIME)

HAWAIIAN SHORT RIBS   CHUTNEY

POTATO PUFFS   FRENCH FRIED ONION RINGS

ASPARAGUS BUNDLES   PARKER HOUSE ROLLS *   BUTTER

PINEAPPLE-MARSHMALLOW SUNDAE   SUGAR WAFERS *   COFFEE

* (Buy these.)

Hawaiian Short Ribs

2 pounds short ribs of beef   1 teaspoon ginger
1 cup soy sauce

Cut meat from bones. Pound to flatten slightly. Mix soy sauce and ginger together; pour over meat. Refrigerate 2 hours.

Asparagus Bundles

1 No. 2 can all-green asparagus
8 green pepper rings
2 tablespoons melted butter

¼ teaspoon salt
⅛ teaspoon pepper
4 slices American cheese

Drain asparagus. Place a quarter of the asparagus bunch inside a pepper ring. Place second ring around lower stalks. Repeat until 4 bundles are made. Season with butter, salt and pepper. Place cheese slice over each bundle.

Potato Puffs and Onion Rings

2 packages each of frozen onion
rings and potato puffs

Broiling Directions

Place puffs and onion rings in broiler pan. Cover with aluminum foil. Remove meat from soy sauce. Place meat on broiler rack. Broil 3 inches below heat source until well browned, about 10 minutes. Baste with soy sauce. Turn meat and baste. Place asparagus bundles on outer edge of broiler rack. Broil 10 minutes longer. Heat rolls below broiler pan. Total broiling time 20 minutes.

Menu 93. Tangy Tongue for Four
(20-MINUTE BROILING TIME)

TANGY TONGUE   DILL PICKLES
SWEET POTATO CAKES   STUFFED TOMATOES
JEWISH PUMPERNICKEL *   BUTTER
PEPPERMINT ICE-BOX CAKE   COFFEE

* (Buy this.)

Tangy Tongue

4 inch-thick slices cooked
   tongue
1½ tablespoons prepared
   mustard

½ cup crushed corn flakes
¼ cup melted butter

Spread slices of tongue with mustard. Mix corn flakes and butter. Dip mustard-covered tongue in buttered flakes. Cover all sides.

Sweet Potato Cakes

1 can sweet potatoes
1 teaspoon onion juice
¼ teaspoon salt

2 tablespoons flour
1½ tablespoons soft butter

Mash sweet potatoes. Add onion juice and salt and mix well. Shape into 4 patties. Dip in flour; spread with soft butter.

Stuffed Tomatoes

4 medium-sized tomatoes
1 tablespoon butter
1 tablespoon finely chopped
   onion

⅛ teaspoon salt
½ cup tiny canned peas
4 thin slices of cheese

Wash tomatoes. Cut slice from stem end. Scoop out tomato pulp and chop. Melt butter; add onion and salt. Simmer until tender but not browned. Combine chopped tomato, onions and peas. Fill tomato shells. Top with cheese half-through broiling.

Broiling Directions

Grease broiler rack. Place potatoes in center, tongue around potatoes, and tomatoes at the outer edge. Place broiler pan so that surface of tomatoes is 4 inches below heat surface. Broil 10 minutes. Turn potatoes and spread with butter. Turn tongue slices. Place cheese on top of stuffed tomatoes. Broil 10 minutes longer, 20 minutes in all.

Peppermint Ice Box Cake

½ pound chocolate-covered peppermints
½ cup evaporated milk
2 tablespoons cold water

2 teaspoons gelatine
1 pint vanilla ice cream
12 ladyfingers

Cut peppermints in quarters. Place evaporated milk and cut peppermints in top of double boiler. Heat over water until mints are dissolved. Sprinkle gelatine over water. When softened, add to hot candy mixture. Stir until gelatine is dissolved. Pour into mixing bowl; add vanilla ice cream and stir until blended. Line loaf pan with double thickness of wax paper. Place 4 ladyfingers in bottom. Pour over half of ice-cream mixture. Place 4 more ladyfingers, then remaining ice-cream mixture and finish by pressing 4 ladyfingers over top of mixture. Chill until firm, about 3 hours.

Menu 94. Broiled Liver for Four

(8-MINUTE BROILING TIME)

BROILED LIVER   SMOTHERED ONIONS

O'BRIEN POTATOES   SPINACH WITH CHOPPED EGG GARNISH

HARD ROLLS *   BUTTER

CRISP SALAD GREENS

WITH CUCUMBER SOUR-CREAM DRESSING (MENU 61)

CANNED FRUIT COCKTAIL   SUGAR COOKIES *   COFFEE

* (Buy these.)

Broiled Liver

1 pound liver, sliced ¾ inch   ½ teaspoon salt
   thick   ⅛ teaspoon pepper
¼ cup salad oil

Wipe liver with paper towel. Mix oil, salt and pepper together.
Brush surface of liver.

Smothered Onions

6 large onions
¼ cup butter

¼ teaspoon salt
⅛ teaspoon pepper

Peel and slice onions. Melt butter in saucepan. Add onions, salt and pepper. Cover tightly. Simmer slowly until onions are tender, about 30 minutes.

O'Brien Potatoes

3 cups finely-diced cooked
    potatoes
3 tablespoons melted butter
⅓ cup finely-chopped onion

⅓ cup chopped pimento
¼ teaspoon salt
⅛ teaspoon pepper
¼ teaspoon paprika

Combine all ingredients and toss lightly until potatoes are buttered and seasonings well blended.

Broiling Directions

Grease broiler pan. Spread onions in center and place liver on top of onions. Arrange potatoes on both ends of broiler pan. Place so that heat source is 3 inches from top of liver. Broil 4 minutes. Turn liver and brush with seasoned oil. Broil 4 minutes longer. Total broiling time 8 minutes.

Menu 95. Lamb Chop Dinner for Four

(10-MINUTE BROILING TIME)

CELERY   MUSTARD PICKLES

LAMB CHOPS

BROWNED POTATO SLICES   PEAS AND CARROTS

BUTTERED TOAST

MINTED PEARS   MARSHMALLOW COOKIES *   TEA

* (Buy these.)

Lamb Chops

2 cups precooked carrots and peas

4 inch-thick lamb chops

Salt

Pepper

8 inch-thick precooked potato slices

¼ cup melted butter

4 canned pear halves

4 tablespoons mint jelly

Broiling Directions

Place peas and carrots in thin layer in bottom of broiler pan. Set rack above vegetables. In the center of broiler rack arrange, close together, lamb chops. Season with salt and pepper. Around the chops place potato slices which have been dipped in melted butter. At each of the four corners place half a pear, center of which has been filled with mint jelly. Preheat broiler for 5 minutes. Place broiler pan so that chops are 2 inches below source of heat. Broil for 5 minutes. Remove pan from the oven. Turn chops and sprinkle with salt and pepper. Turn potato slices over and brush with butter. Return to broiler and continue broiling for 5 minutes. Heat rolls below the broiler pan. Total broiling time 10 minutes.

Note: Vegetables below the meat will be seasoned with meat juices and heated through. Pear halves will be hot but not browned.

Menu 96. Lamb-Bacon Patties for Four

(18-MINUTE BROILING TIME)

LAMB-BACON PATTIES   PEARS AU GRATIN

RICE CAKES   BUTTERED CORN

HAWAIIAN DESSERT   GINGERSNAPS *   COFFEE

* (Buy these.)

Lamb-Bacon Patties

½ pound sliced bacon
1½ pounds ground lamb
    shoulder
1 tablespoon Worcestershire
    sauce

1 cup crushed corn flakes
3 tablespoons milk
¼ teaspoon salt
⅛ teaspoon pepper

Arrange bacon on wax paper so that slices overlap. Mix together lamb, Worcestershire sauce, corn flakes, milk, salt and pepper. Spread over bacon. Roll up so that ends of bacon are rolled into meat. Wrap tightly in wax paper. Chill. Remove from refrigerator; place wooden picks through roll at 1-inch intervals. Cut roll into inch-thick slices between wooden picks.

Rice Cakes

1½ cups cooked rice
1 egg yolk
¼ teaspoon salt
⅛ teaspoon pepper

1/16 teaspoon nutmeg
⅓ cup fine cracker crumbs
2 tablespoons butter, melted

To rice add egg yolk, salt, pepper and nutmeg. Shape into 4 patties. Press into crumbs on all sides. Brush well with butter.

Buttered Corn

1 (No. 1½ flat) can whole-
  kernel corn

1 tablespoon melted butter
⅛ teaspoon pepper

Drain corn. Season with butter and pepper.

Pears au Gratin

4 canned pear halves
2 tablespoons mayonnaise

4 thin slices sharp cheese

Drain pears and dry on paper towel. Spread with mayonnaise. Top each half with slice of cheese.

Broiling Directions

Grease broiler pan. Place rice cakes at one end and corn at the other. Set rack over corn and rice. Place lamb in center of rack. Set pan so that top of patties is 2½ inches from heat source. Broil 9 minutes. Turn patties. Place pears on outer edge of rack and broil 9 minutes longer. Total broiling time 18 minutes.

Hawaiian Dessert

3 oranges
2½ cups (No. 2 can) crushed
  pineapple

¼ cup sugar
½ cup shredded coconut
4 maraschino cherries

Peel and slice oranges; add pineapple (not drained), sugar and coconut. Mix and chill. Cut cherries to form poinsettias and use as garnish.

Menu 97. Ham-Asparagus Rolls for Four

(10-MINUTE BROILING TIME)

HAM-ASPARAGUS ROLLS   BREAD AND BUTTER PICKLES

POTATO CHIPS

BUTTERED CAULIFLOWER

BANANAS IN BACON   MELBA TOAST *   BUTTER

FIG FRITTERS WITH BUTTER SAUCE   COFFEE

* (Buy this.)

Ham-Asparagus Rolls

16 stalks jumbo asparagus,
    cooked
8 slices boiled ham

2 tablespoons melted butter
4 slices American cheese

On 2 overlapping slices of ham place 4 stalks cooked asparagus. Dredge with butter. Place cheese slice on top and roll ham. Fasten with wooden picks. Repeat to make 4 rolls.

Buttered Cauliflower

1 head cauliflower
1 quart boiling water
1 teaspoon salt

2 tablespoons butter
2 tablespoons fine bread crumbs

Wash cauliflower. Separate into flowerets. Cook in boiling salted water until just tender. Drain. Pour butter over flowerets. Sprinkle with crumbs.

Bananas in Bacon

4 small yellow bananas
2 tablespoons butter

4 strips bacon

Peel bananas. Broil with butter. Wrap in bacon. Fasten with wooden picks.

Broiling Directions

Spread cauliflower over greased broiler pan and set rack over it. Arrange ham rolls in center of rack and bananas around the edge. Place broiler pan so that top of ham rolls is 3 inches from heat source. Broil 5 minutes. Turn ham rolls and bananas. Broil 5 minutes longer. Total broiling time 10 minutes.

Fig Fritters

1 cup flour	1 egg
½ teaspoon salt	⅔ cup sour cream
1½ teaspoons baking powder	¼ teaspoon grated lemon rind
½ teaspoon baking soda	¾ cup finely-cut figs
1 tablespoon sugar	

Sift together flour, salt, baking powder, soda and sugar. Beat egg; add sour cream and lemon rind to egg. Add figs and liquids to sifted dry ingredients. Mix until just blended but not smooth. Drop into hot fat (365°). Fry until golden brown, turning once. Drain and serve with butter sauce.

BUTTER SAUCE

¼ cup butter	1 cup boiling water
2 tablespoons flour	1 tablespoon lemon juice
2 tablespoons sugar	

Melt butter; add flour and sugar. Add water slowly and bring to a boil. Add lemon juice and place over hot water. Cover. Keep heat low until serving time.

Menu 98. Ham Rollups for Four
(15-MINUTE BROILING TIME)

HAM-AND-SWEET POTATO ROLLUPS

MINTED PINEAPPLE STICKS   BUTTERED BROCCOLI

LETTUCE HEARTS AND CHILI SAUCE DRESSING (MENU 50)

CODDLED APPLES   RAISIN COOKIES *   COFFEE

* (Buy these.)

Ham-and-Sweet Potato Rollups

1 pound ground ham
½ cup bread crumbs
1 egg, beaten
2 tablespoons grated onion

¼ cup tomato catsup
1 can (No. 1½ flat) sweet
    potatoes

Mix together ham, crumbs, egg, onion and catsup. Roll out ½ inch thick on wax paper. Mash sweet potatoes and spread over ham. Roll up like a jelly roll. Cut in 1½-inch-thick slices.

Minted Pineapple Sticks

4 pineapple sticks, fresh or
    canned
1 tablespoon chopped mint

2 tablespoons brown sugar
2 tablespoons melted butter

Roll pineapple sticks in chopped mint; sprinkle with half the sugar and butter.

Buttered Broccoli

2 cups cooked broccoli   ¼ teaspoon salt
2 tablespoons melted butter

Broiling Directions

Grease broiler pan. Place broccoli at one end of pan. Pour butter over broccoli and sprinkle with salt. Place pineapple sticks at opposite end of pan. Cover with broiler rack. Place ham roll-ups in center of rack. Set broiler pan so that meat surface is 3 inches below heat source. Broil 8 minutes. Remove rack. Turn pineapple sticks and cover with remaining sugar and butter. Turn broccoli. Replace rack. Turn ham and broil 7 minutes longer. Total broiling time 15 minutes.

Coddled Apples

1 cup sugar   4 large apples
1 cup water   ½ teaspoon nutmeg

Mix sugar and water in large saucepan. Let stand until sugar is dissolved. Pare apples. Cut each in eight pieces. Remove core. Drop into sirup; add nutmeg and bring to a boil. Cook slowly until apples are tender. Do not stir. Chill and serve.

Menu 99. Sweetbreads and Ham
for Four
(7½-MINUTE BROILING TIME)

SWEETBREADS AND HAM   GREEN TOMATO PICKLES
CANDIED SWEET POTATOES   WAX BEANS O'BRIEN
TOSSED SALAD WITH ROQUEFORT DRESSING (MENU 54)
BREAD STICKS *   BUTTER
BRANDIED GRAPEFRUIT   COFFEE

* (Buy these.)

Sweetbreads and Ham

2 pairs sweetbreads
1 quart boiling water
1 tablespoon vinegar
1 teaspoon salt

3 tablespoons melted butter
4 quarter-inch slices ham
⅛ teaspoon pepper

Soak sweetbreads in cold water for 10 minutes. Drain and cut in half; remove all membrane. Plunge in boiling water; add vinegar and salt. Simmer 15 minutes. Drain and dry on paper towels. Roll in melted butter. Place each piece on a ham slice and sprinkle with pepper.

Candied Sweet Potatoes

¼ cup honey

¼ teaspoon nutmeg

1 can (No. 1½ flat) sweet potatoes

Combine honey and nutmeg. Dip sweet potatoes in honey mixture. Place at one end of greased broiler pan. Pour remaining honey over potatoes.

Wax Beans O'Brien

2½ cups (No. 2 can) cut wax beans

2 tablespoons butter

¼ cup chopped onions

¼ cup chopped pimento

Drain wax beans. Melt butter; add onions and simmer until tender. Add pimento and drained wax beans and blend. Pile at one end of greased broiler pan.

Broiling Directions

Place broiler rack over sweet potatoes and beans in pan. Place ham and sweetbreads on broiler rack. Set rack so that top of sweetbreads is 3 inches below heat source. Broil 6 minutes. Remove sweetbreads and ham. Remove rack and raise broiler pan 1 inch. Broil 1½ minutes longer. Total broiling time 7½ minutes.

Menu 100. Broiled Breakfast for Four

(8-MINUTE BROILING TIME)

HOT GRAPEFRUIT
CORNED BEEF HASH AND POACHED EGGS
CRISP BACON
TOASTED ENGLISH MUFFINS   JAM   BUTTER   COFFEE

Grapefruit

2 grapefruit   1 tablespoon butter
¼ cup brown sugar

Cut grapefruit in half; remove seeds. Cut around sections, taking care not to cut membrane. Top with sugar and butter.

Corned Beef Hash and Poached Eggs

2 cans (No. 2) corned beef
  hash
4 eggs

¼ teaspoon salt
2 teaspoons butter
4 strips bacon

Shape hash into 4 nests. Drop egg in center of each. Sprinkle egg
with salt. Dot with butter. Cut bacon in half and cross two pieces
over each egg.

Toasted English Muffins

4 English muffins

4 teaspoons soft butter

Tear muffins in half. Do not use knife. Spread with soft butter

Broiling Directions

Place buttered muffins on outer edges of broiler pan. Cover with
rack. Place hash nests in center of greased rack and grapefruit at
outer edges of rack. Set broiler pan so that surface of grapefruit
is 3 inches from heat source. Broil 4 minutes. Remove grapefruit
and broil 4 minutes longer. Total broiling time 8 minutes.

Menu 101. Baked Beans for Six
(10-MINUTE BROILING TIME)

BAKED BEANS WITH BACON   CHILI SAUCE
BROWN BREAD
BREADED TOMATO SLICES
CRISP SALAD GREENS
WITH CUCUMBER SOUR-CREAM DRESSING (MENU 61)
COCONUT SQUARES   CHILLED APPLESAUCE   COFFEE

Baked Beans with Bacon

1 can (No. 3) baked beans   6 strips bacon
1 can (No. 3) brown bread   ⅓ cup chili sauce
3 tablespoons butter

Slice brown bread and spread with butter. Pile beans on brown bread. Cut bacon strips in half and cross 2 pieces over beans. Top with chili sauce.

Breaded Tomato Slices

4 tomatoes   1 egg
¼ cup flour   1 tablespoon water
½ teaspoon salt   ½ cup fine bread crumbs
⅛ teaspoon pepper

Cut tomatoes into ⅓-inch-thick slices. Mix flour, salt and pepper. Beat egg and water together. Dip tomato slices first in seasoned flour, then in egg and crumbs.

Coconut Squares

3 inch-thick slices pound cake
1 can sweetened condensed
   milk

1½ cups shredded moist coconut

Cut each slice of cake in half. Dip in condensed milk, then in coconut.

Broiling Directions

Grease broiler pan. Lay coconut squares at one end of pan and tomato slices at other end of pan. Cover with broiler rack. Place bean sandwiches on rack. Place broiler pan so tops of sandwiches are 3 inches below heat source. Broil 10 minutes. Remove sandwiches and tomatoes. If coconut is not lightly browned, broil 1 minute longer.

Serving Directions

Place hot coconut squares on plate. Pile chilled applesauce over each square.

INDEX